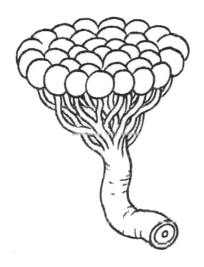

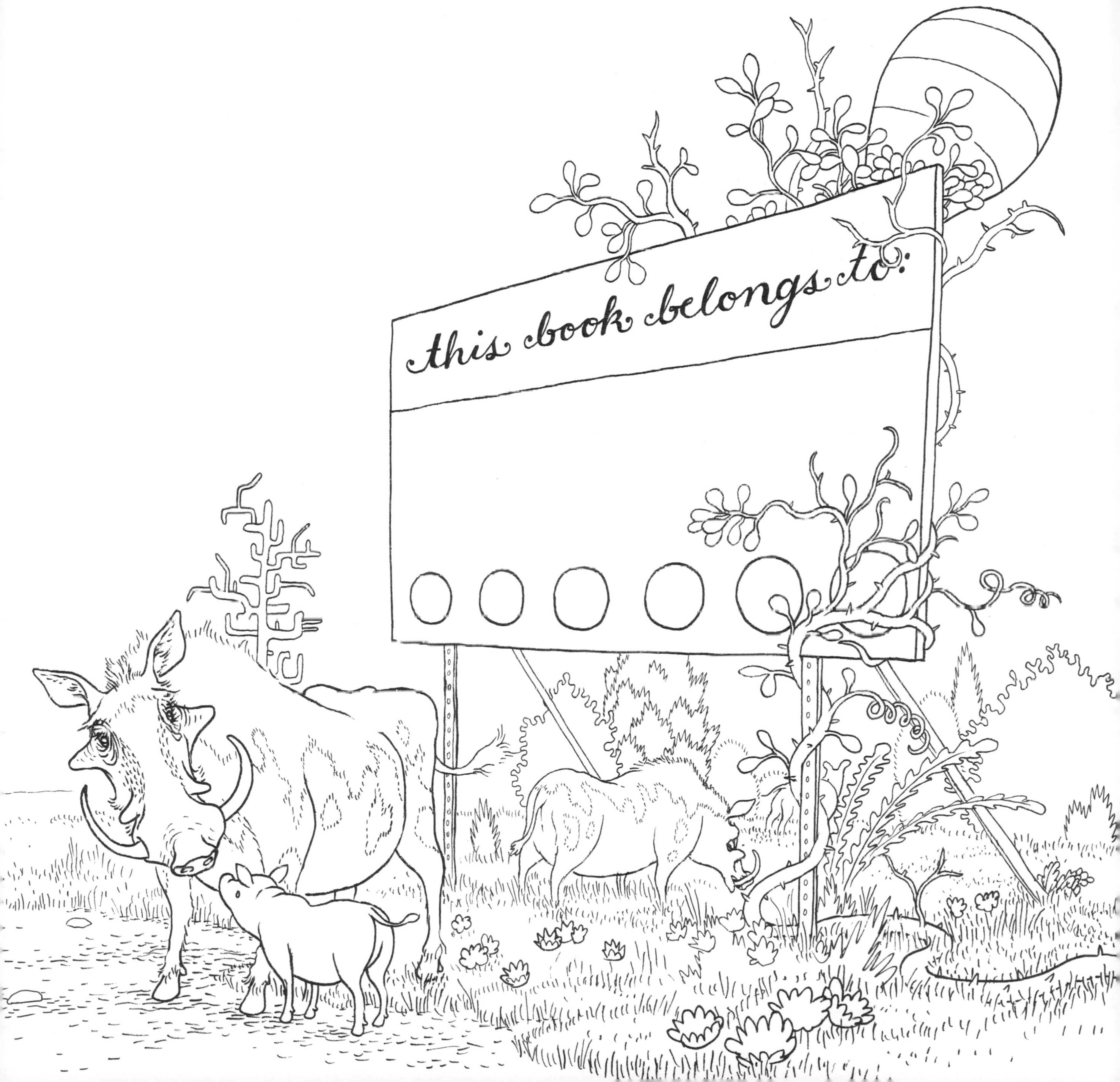
this book belongs to:

andersbrekhusnilsen.com
drawnandquarterly.com

First edition: November 2016
Printed in China
10 9 8 7 6 5 4 3 2 1

Library and Archives Canada Cataloguing in Publication
Nilsen, Anders, 1973–, artist
   A Walk in Eden: A colouring book / by Anders Nilsen.
ISBN 978-1-77046-266-3 (paperback)
1. Natural history—Pictorial works. 2. Botany—Pictorial works.
3. Coloring books. I. Title.
QH46.N55 2016   578.022'2   C2016-900990-4

Published in the USA by Drawn & Quarterly,
a client publisher of Farrar, Straus and Giroux. Orders: 888.330.8477

Published in Canada by Drawn & Quarterly,
a client publisher of Raincoast Books. Orders: 800.663.5714

Published in the United Kingdom by Drawn & Quarterly,
a client publisher of Publishers Group UK. Orders: info@pguk.co.uk

A WALK IN EDEN

anders nilsen

drawn and quarterly

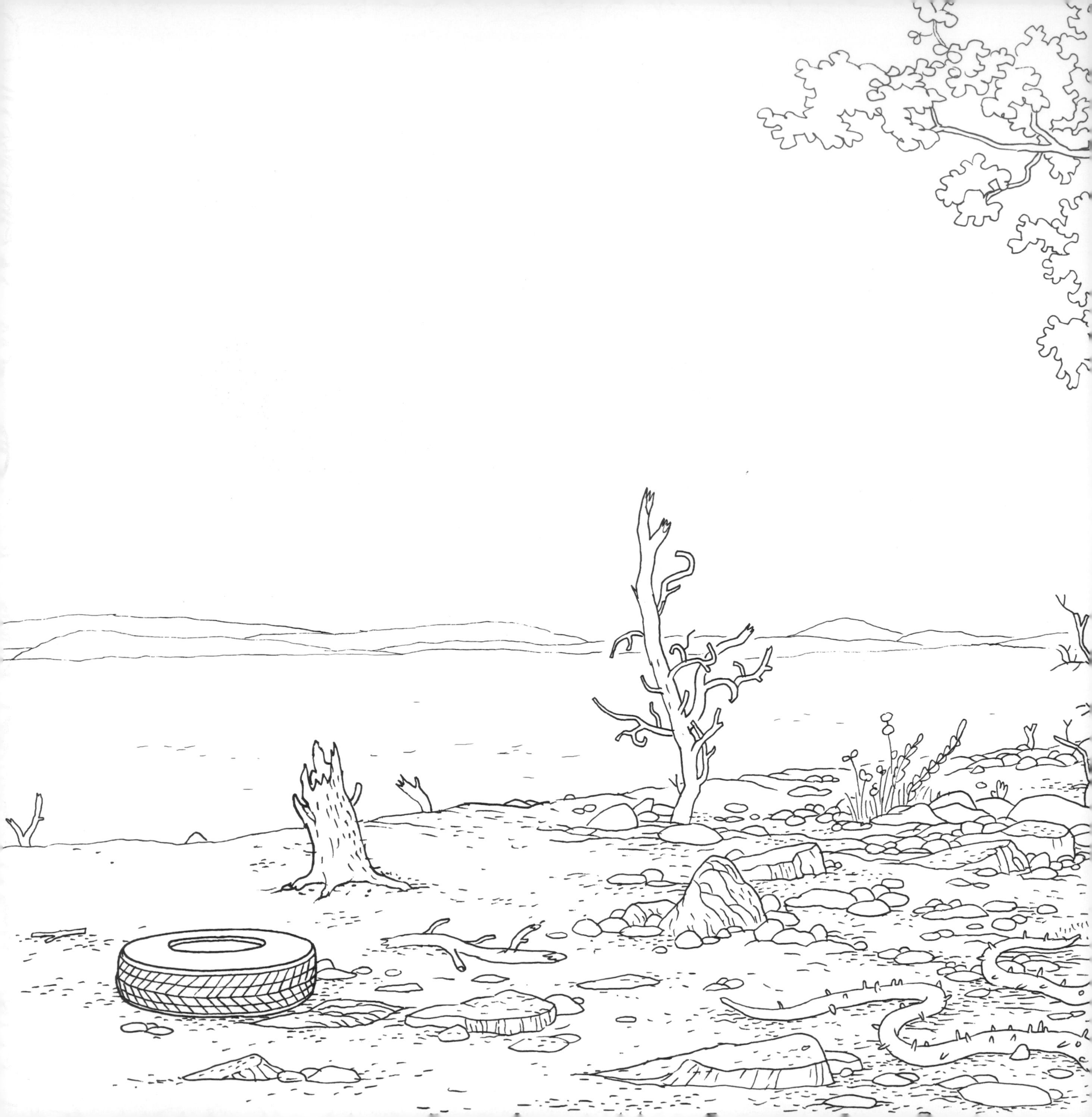

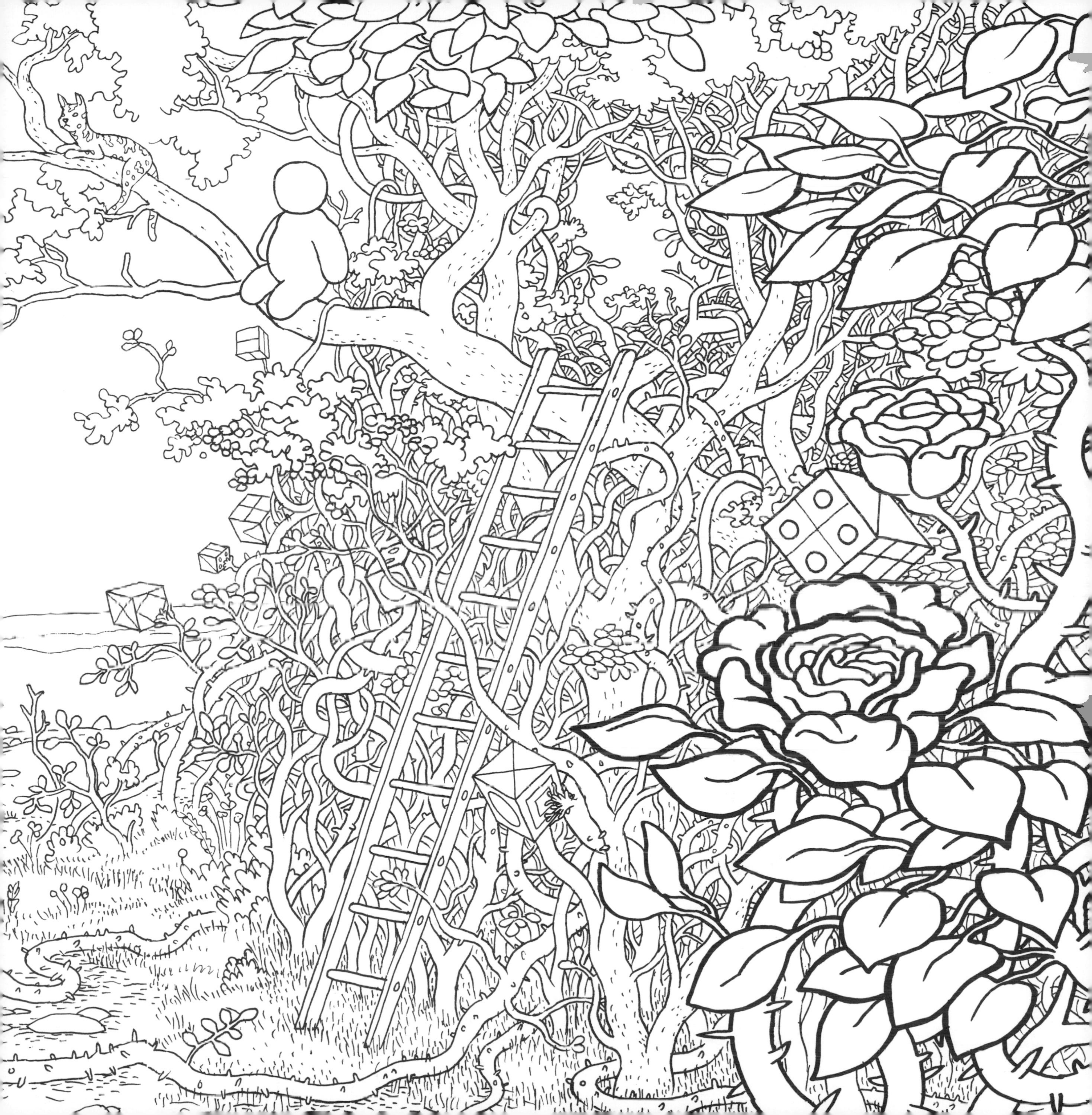

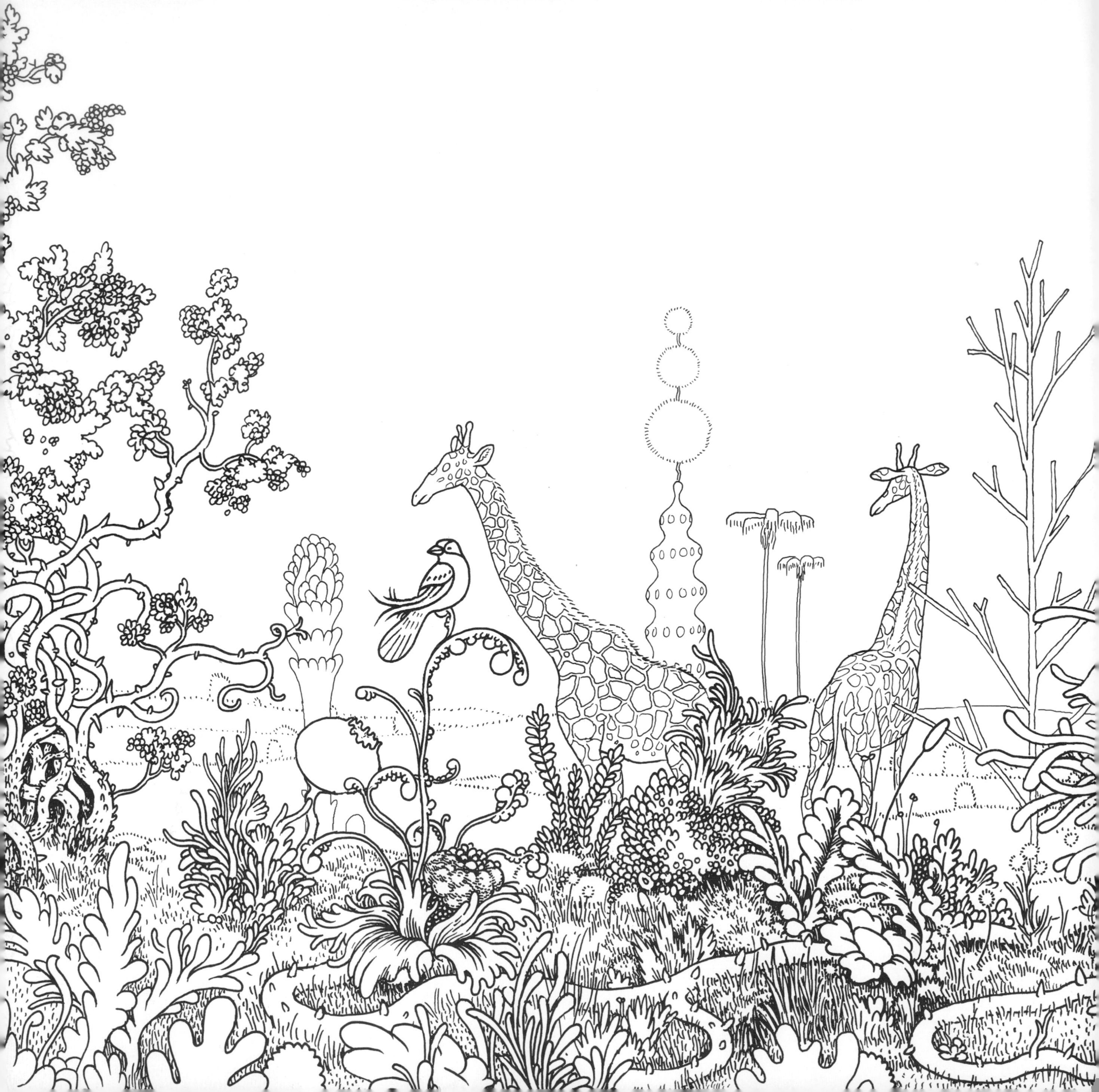

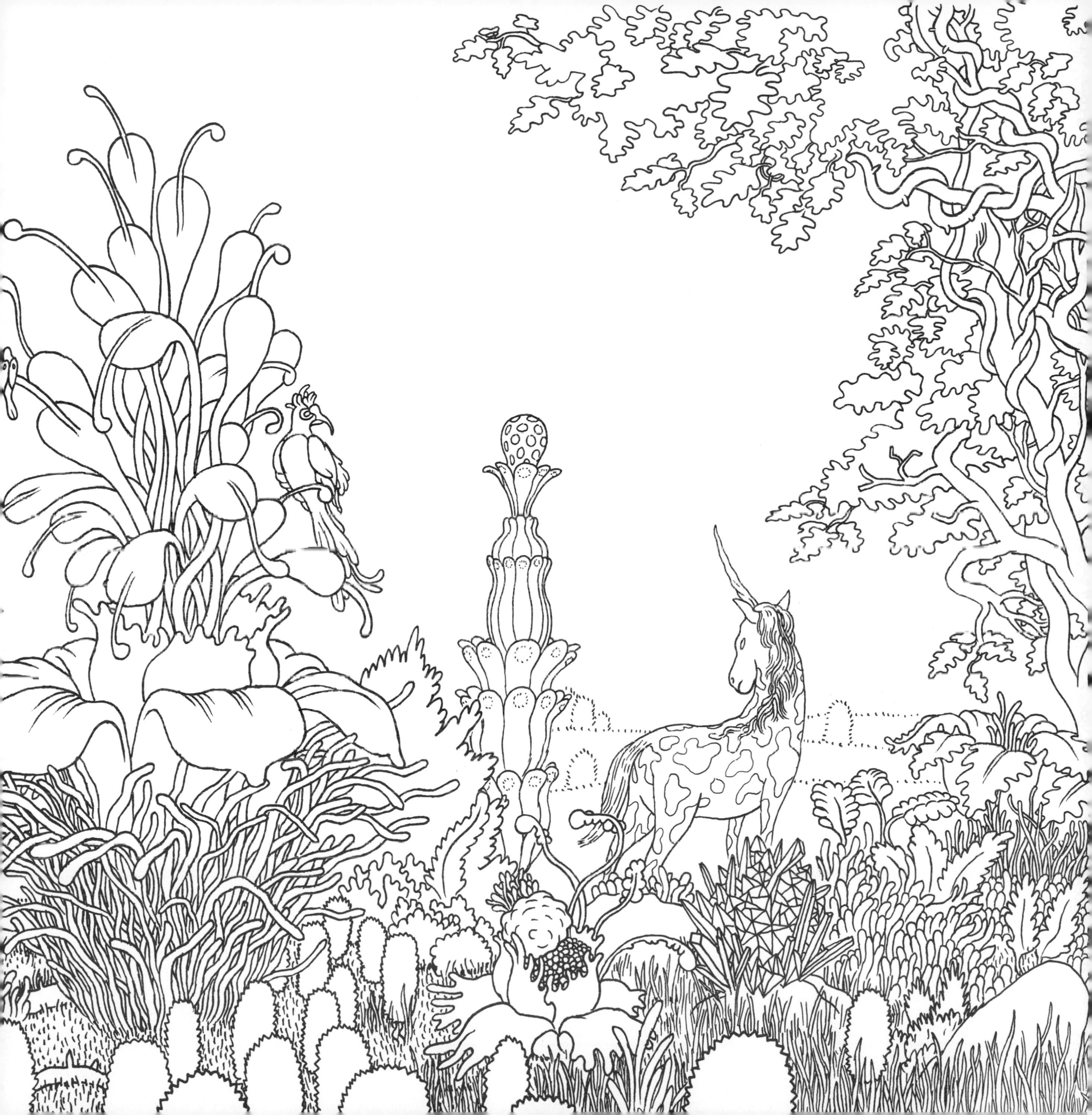

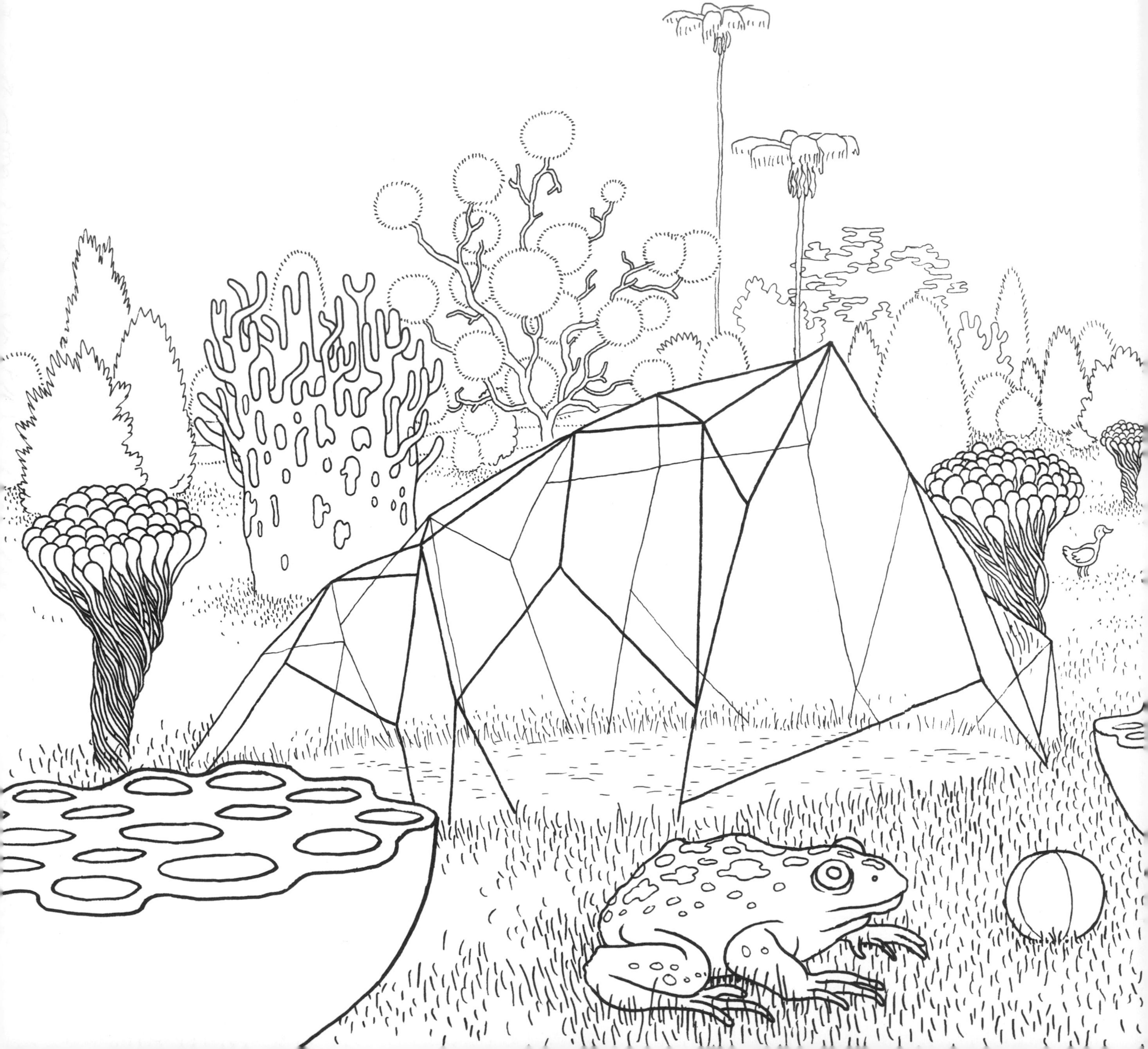

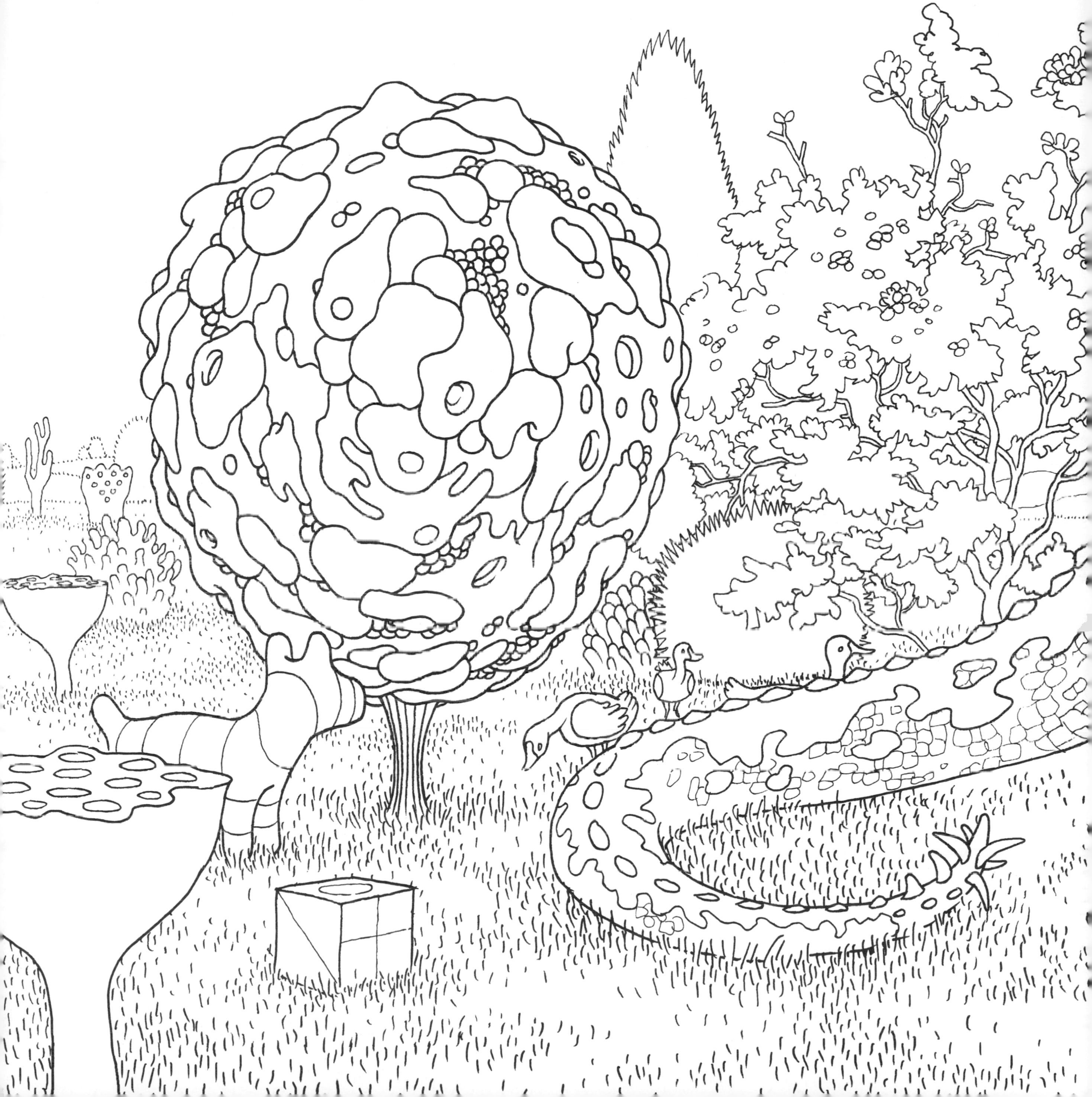

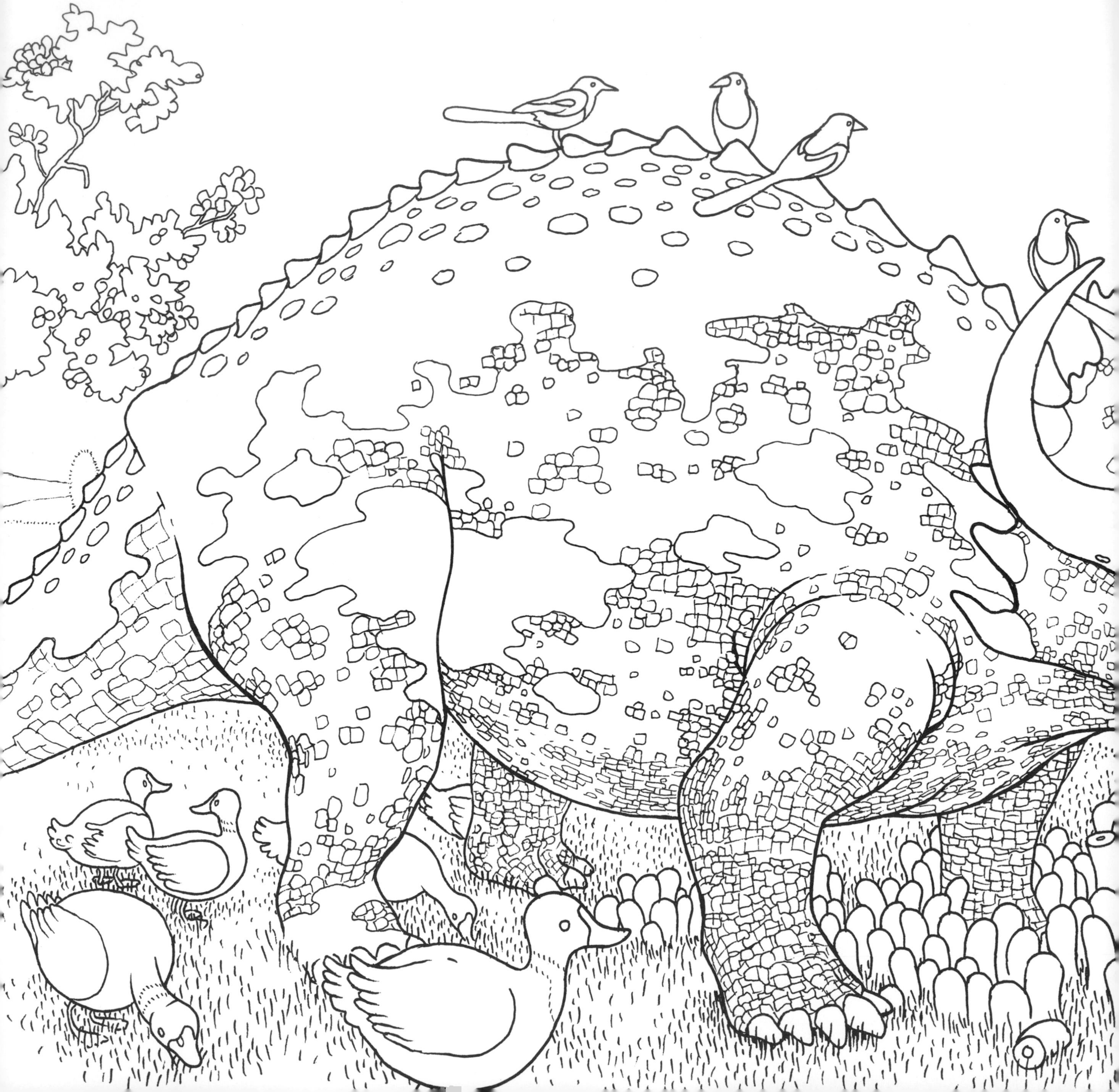

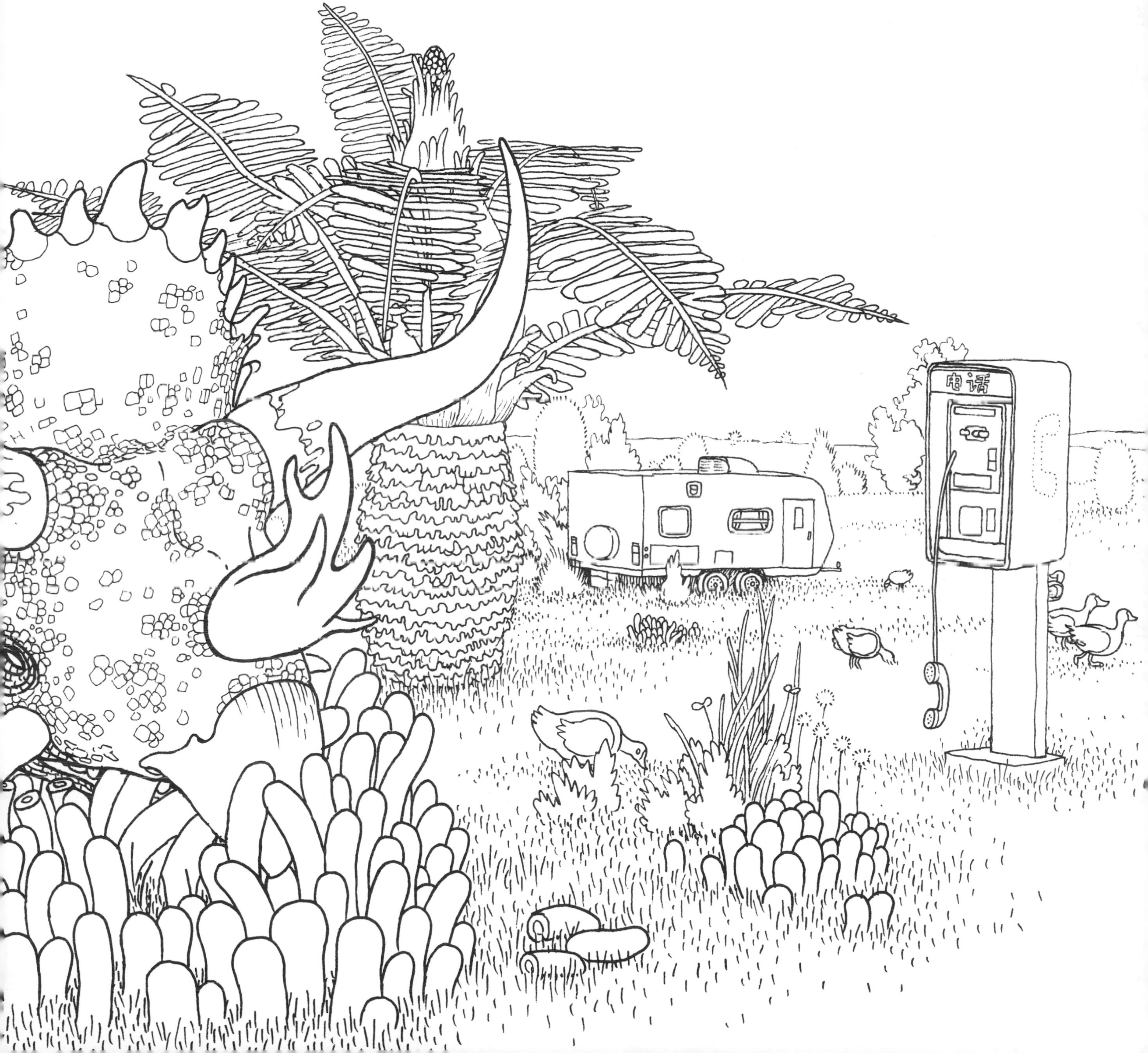
电话

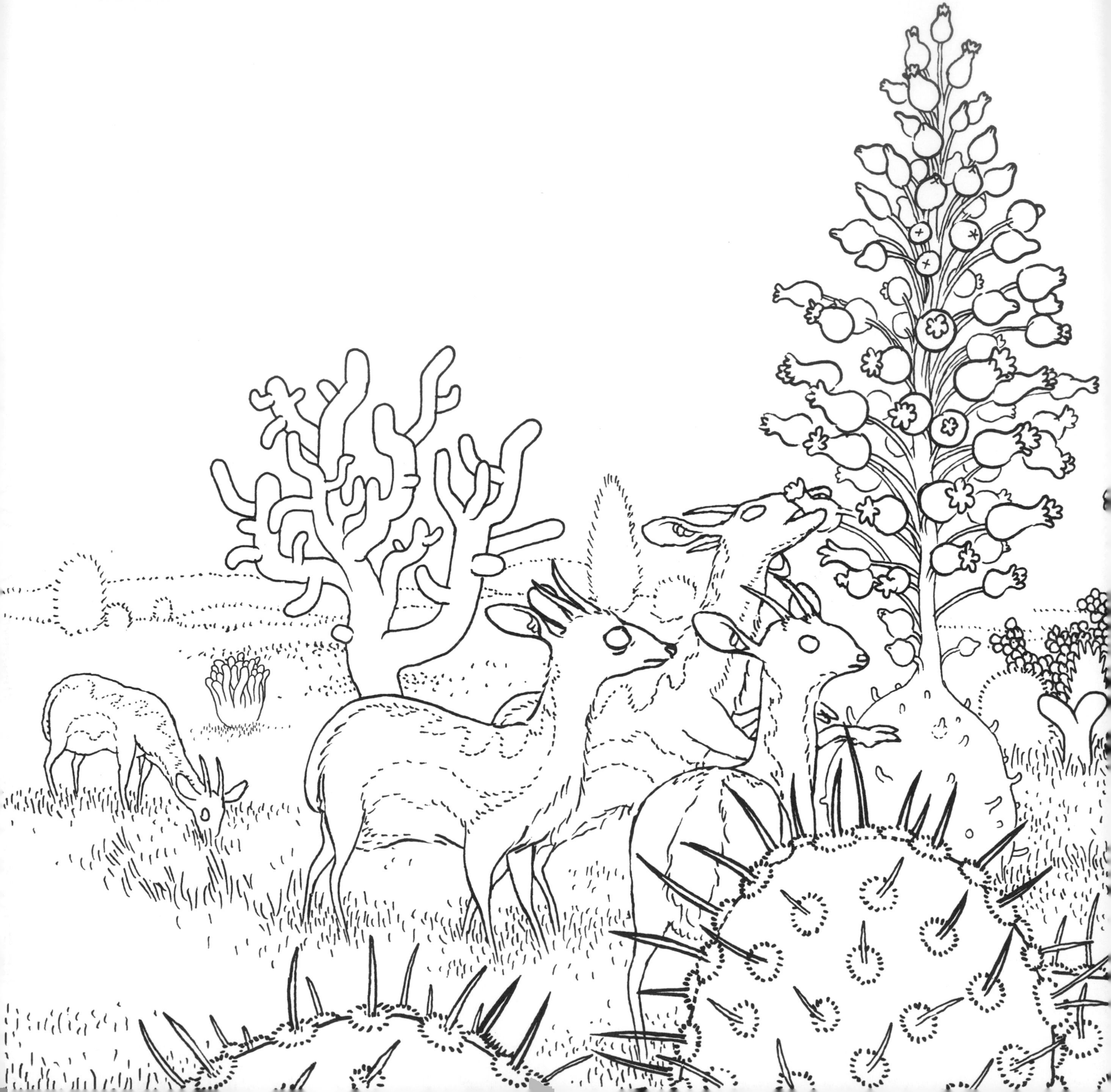

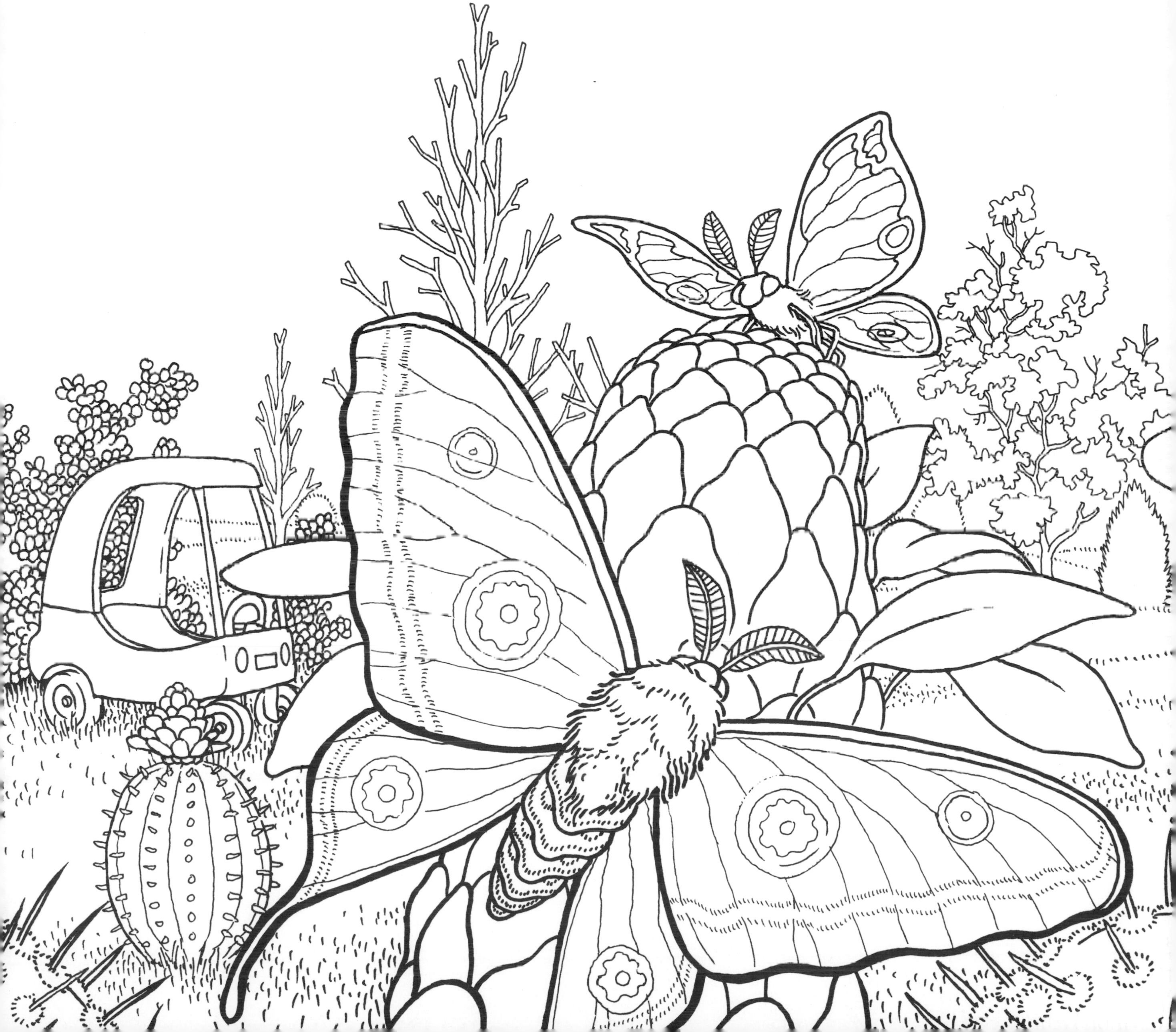

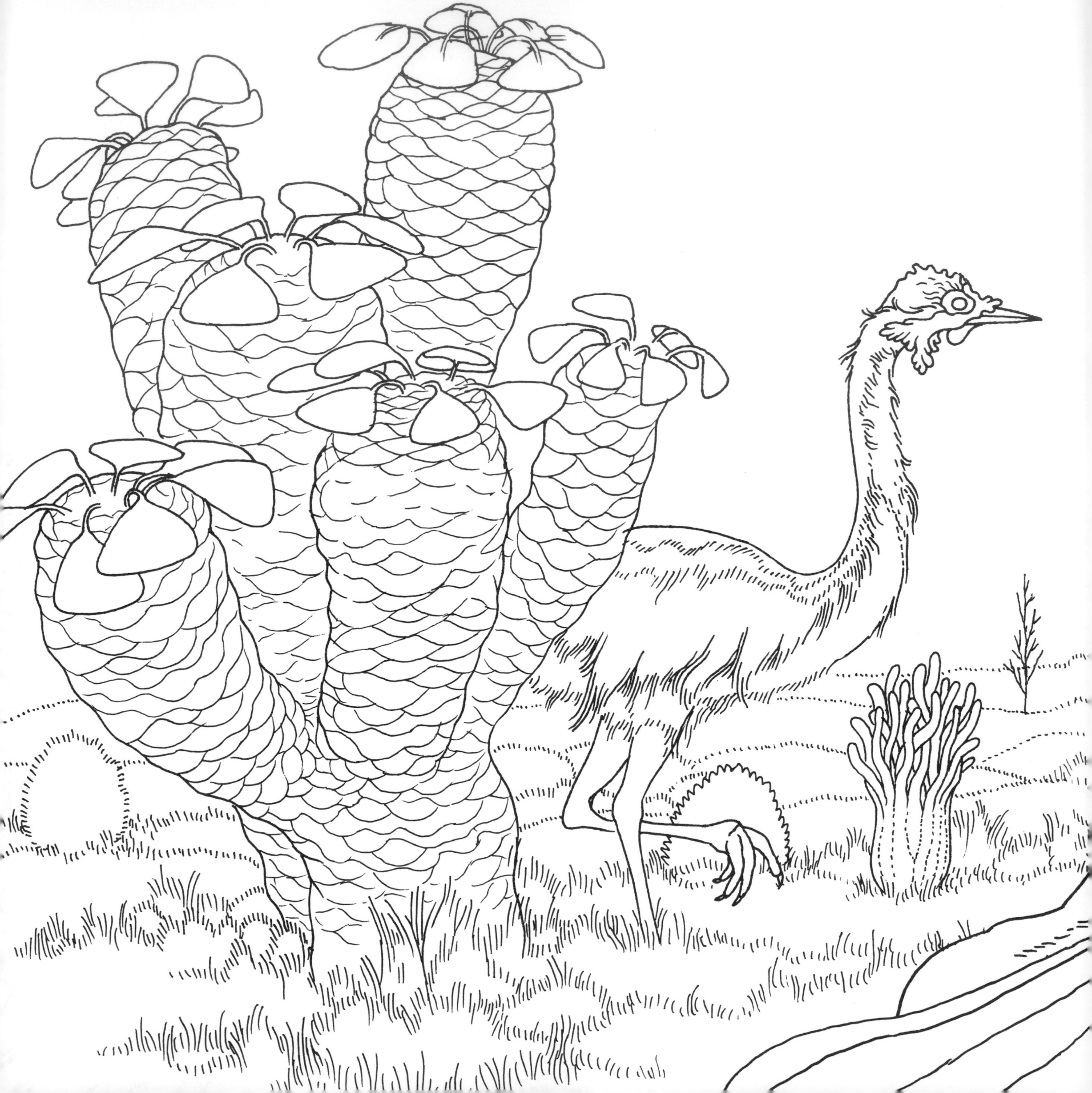

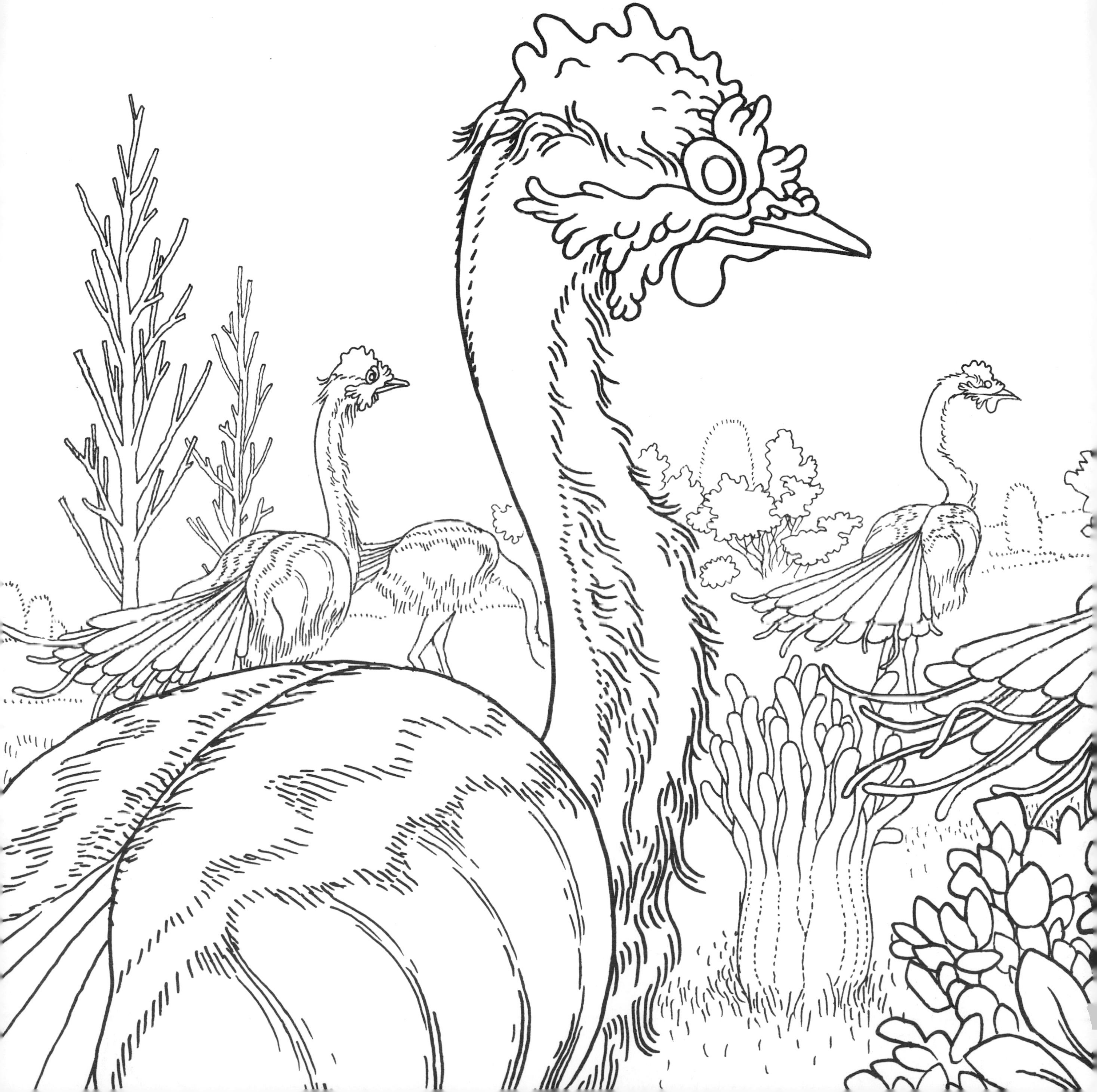

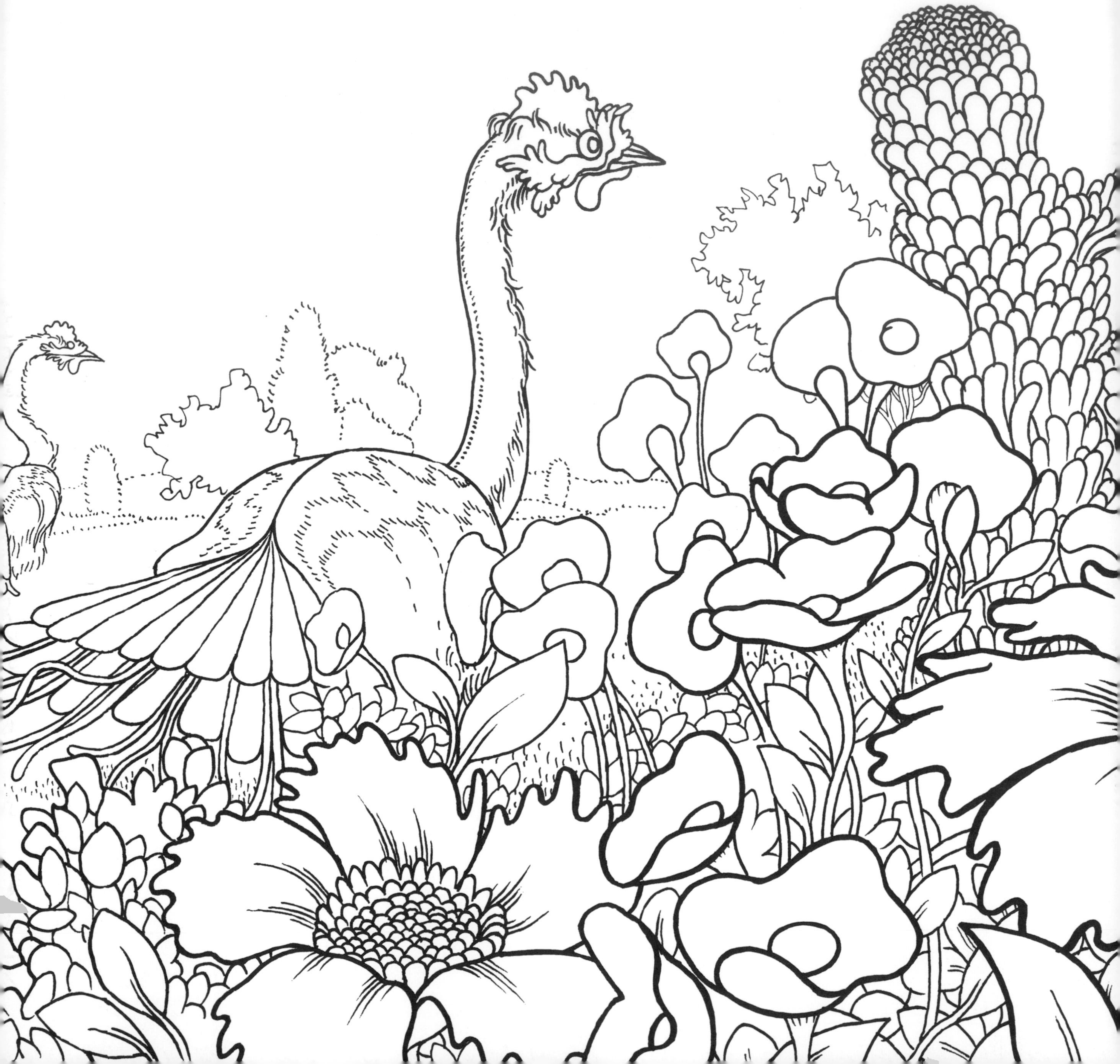

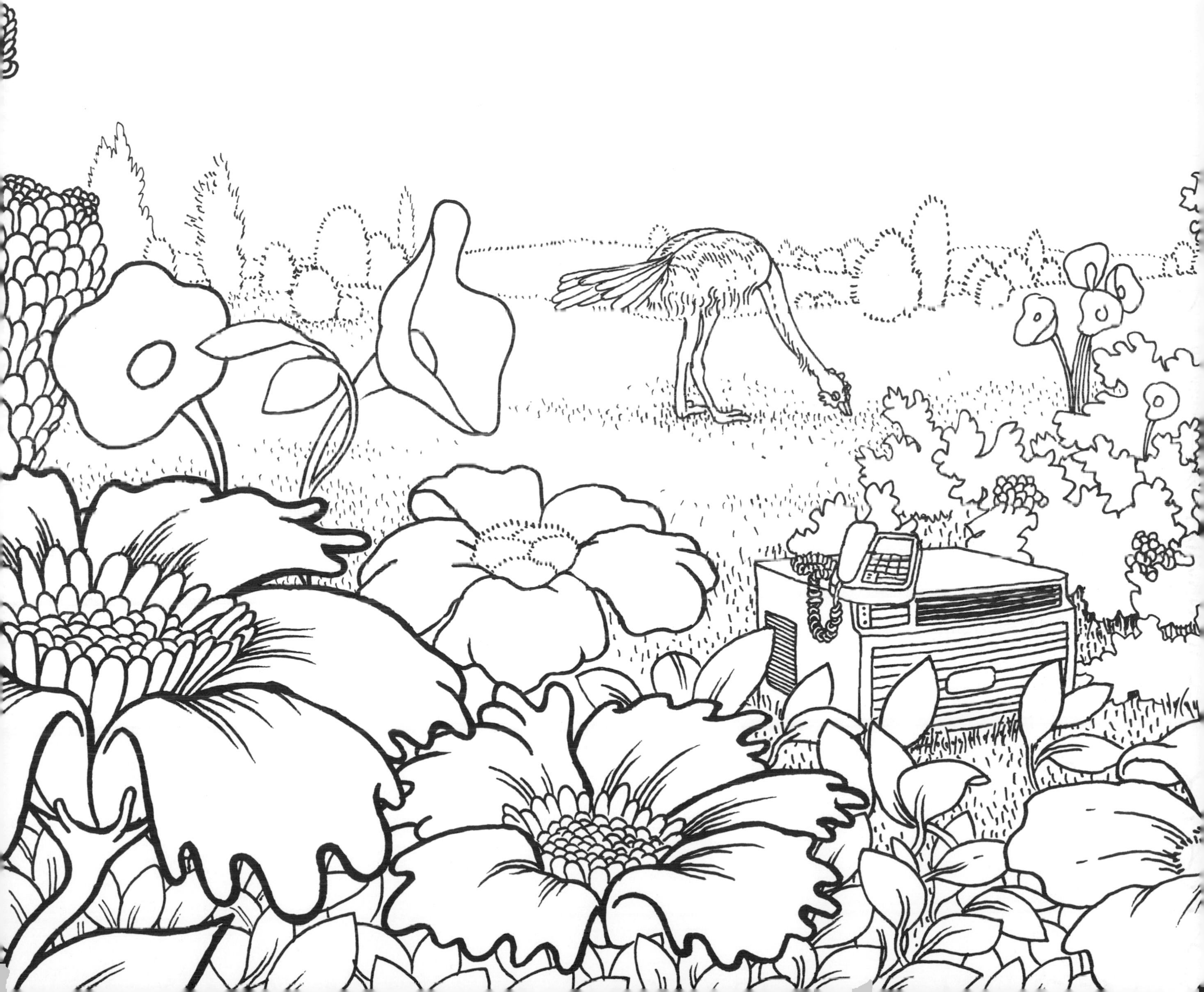

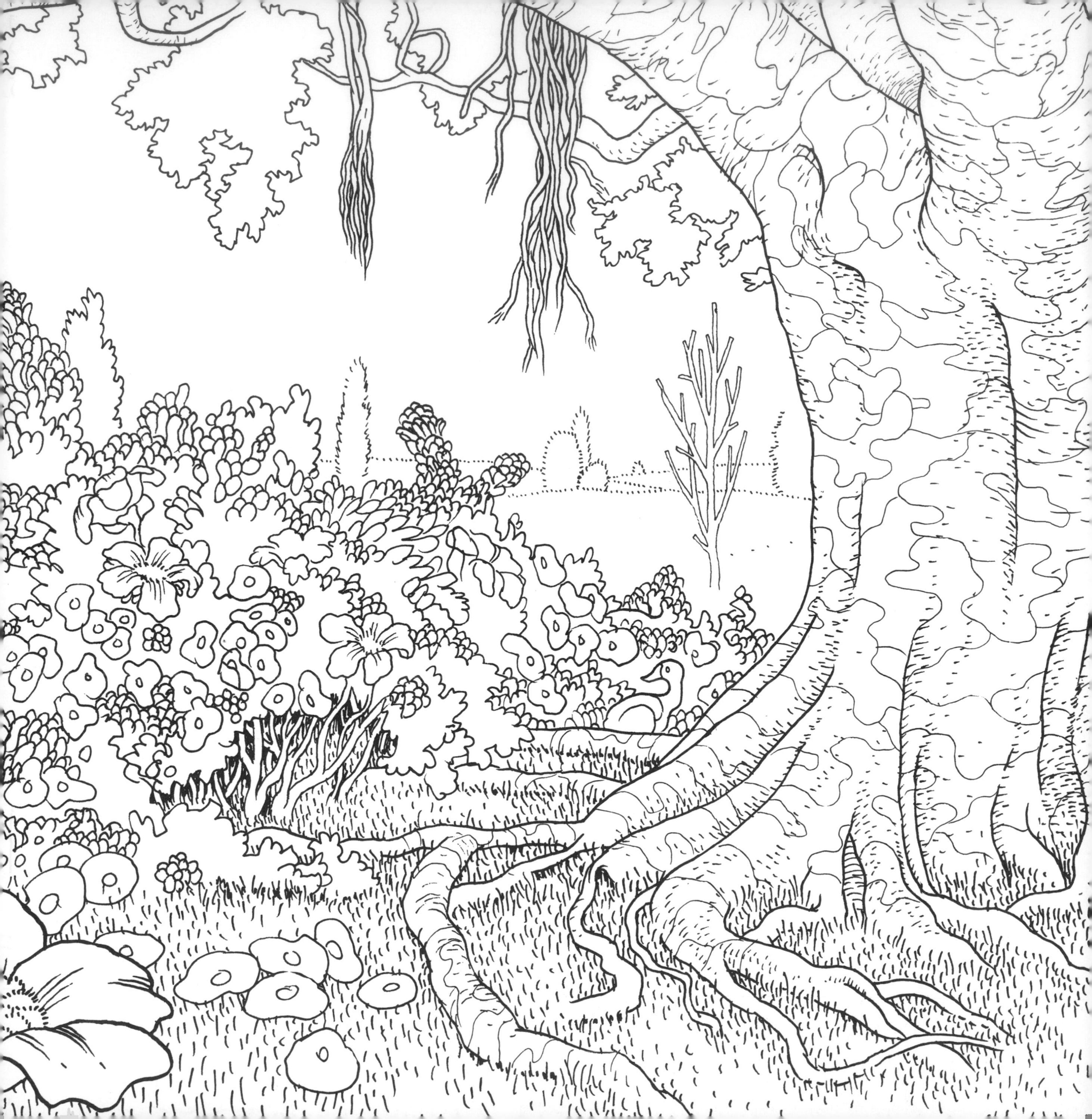

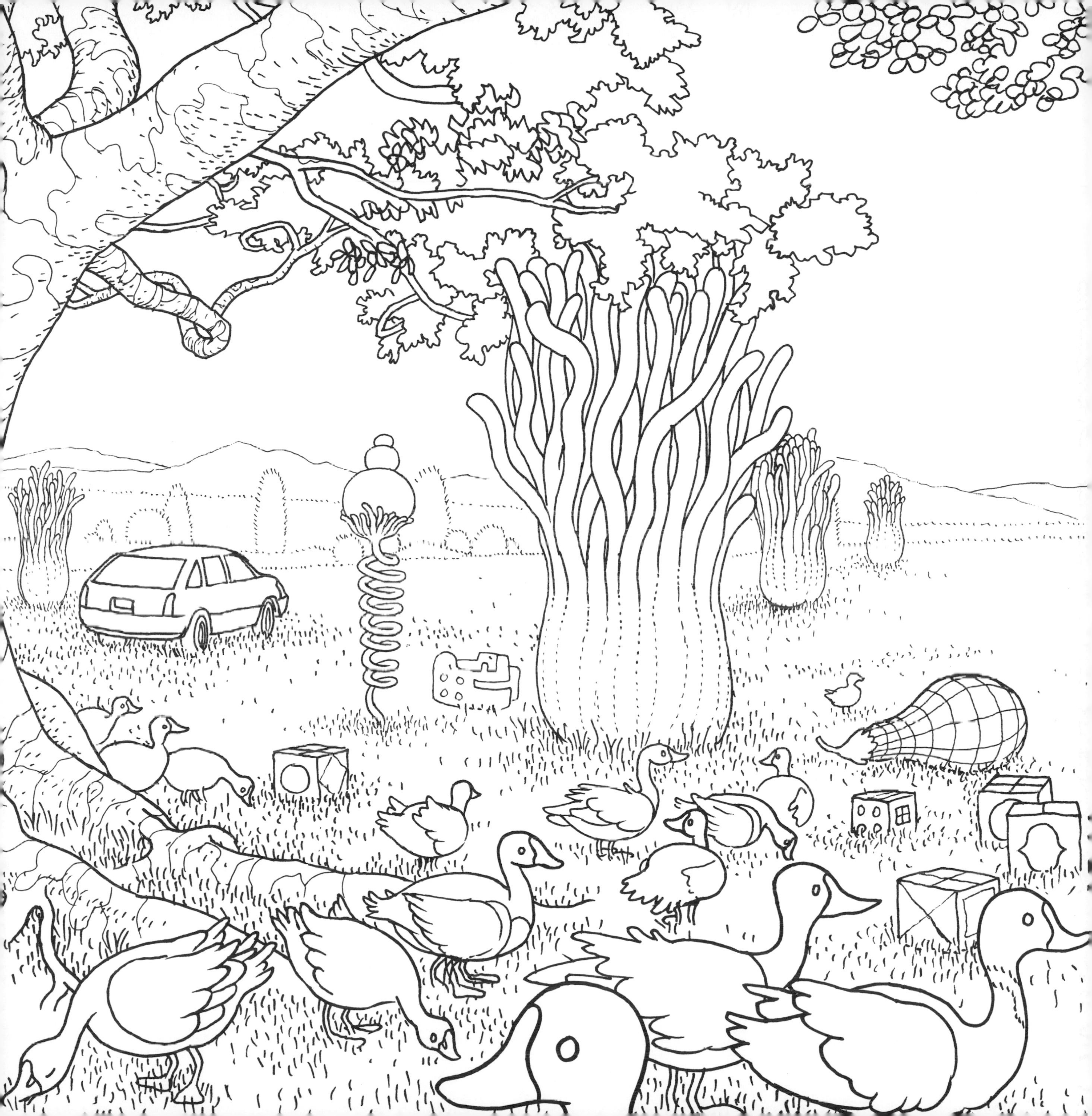

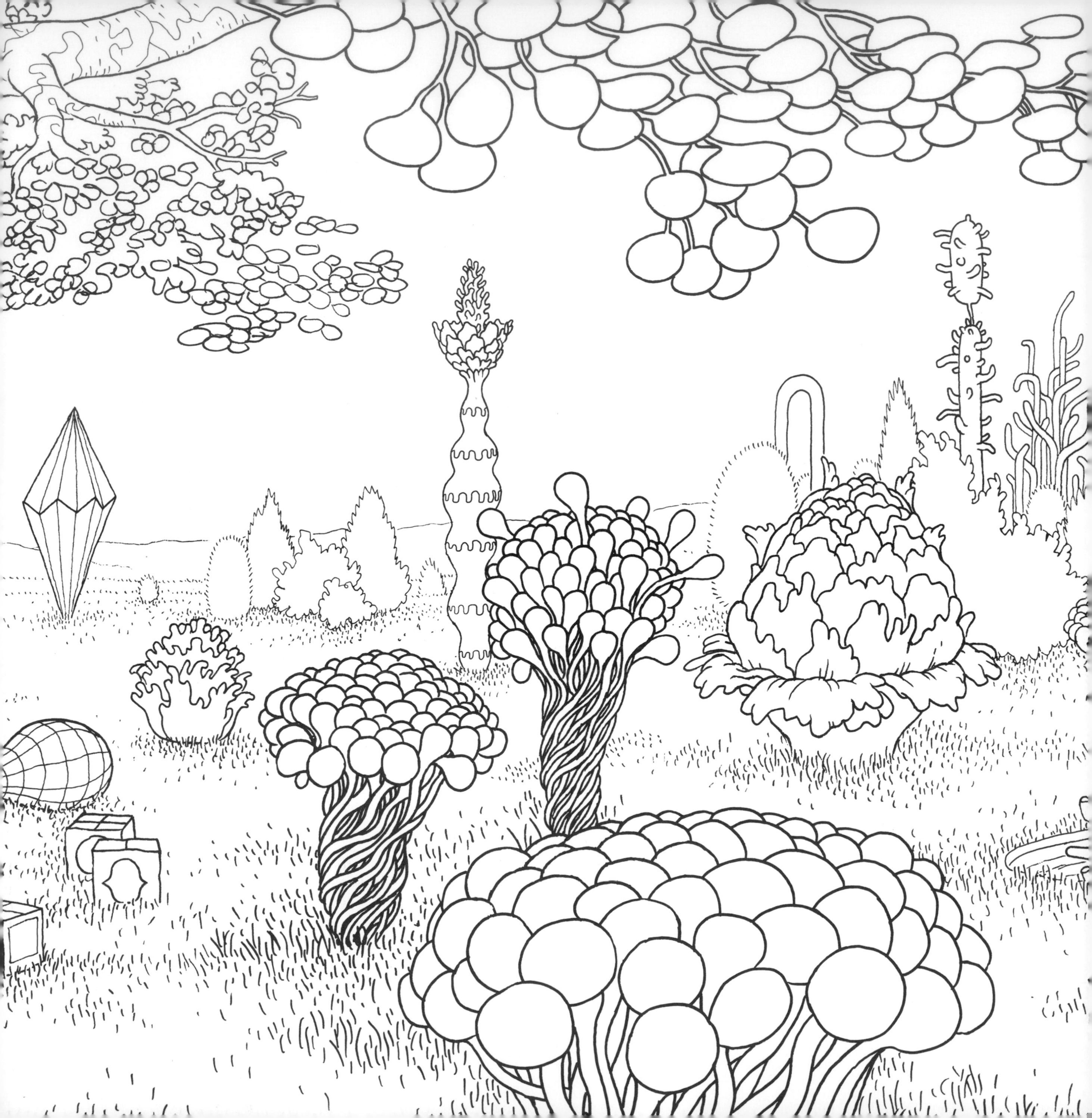

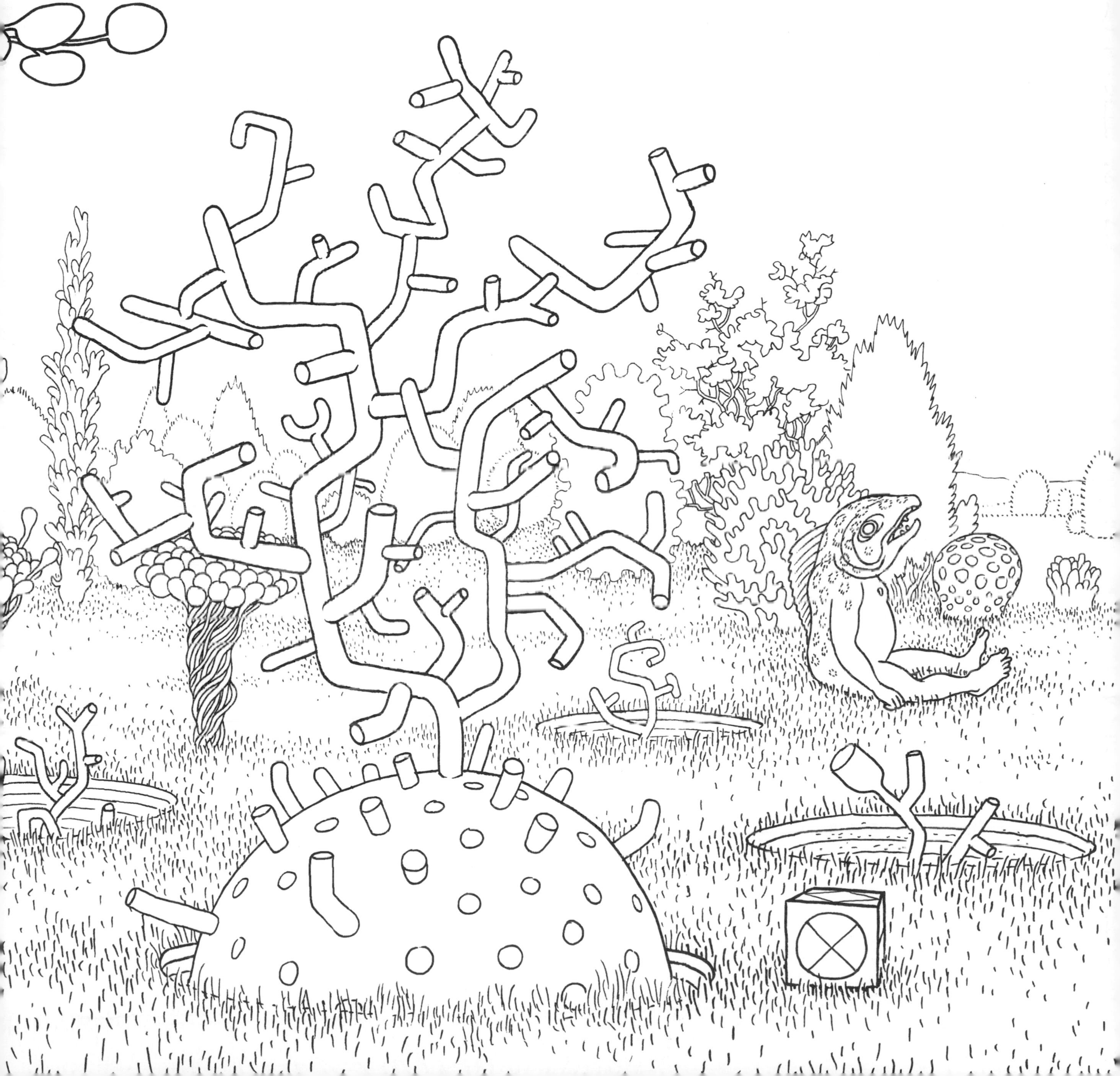

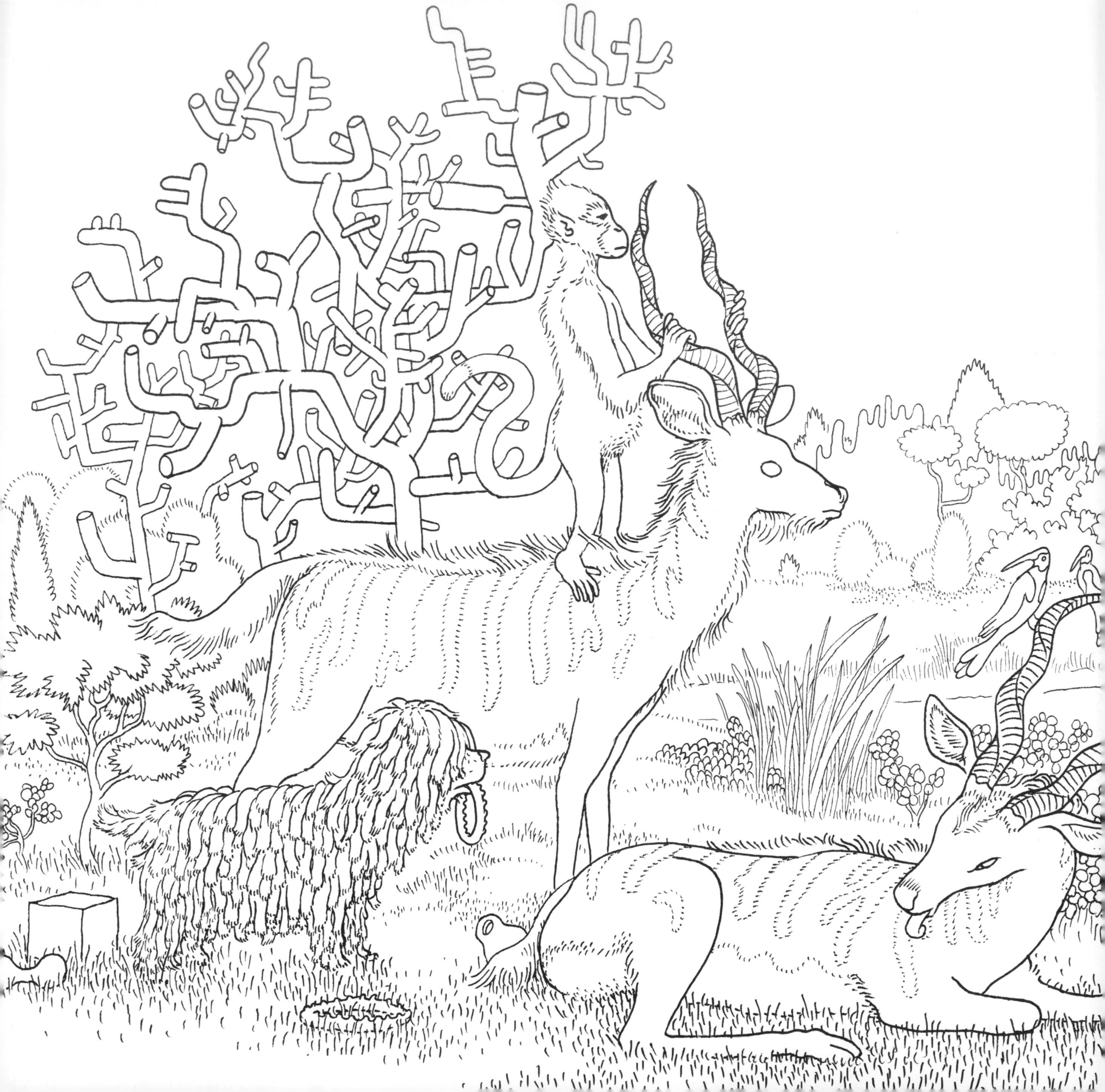

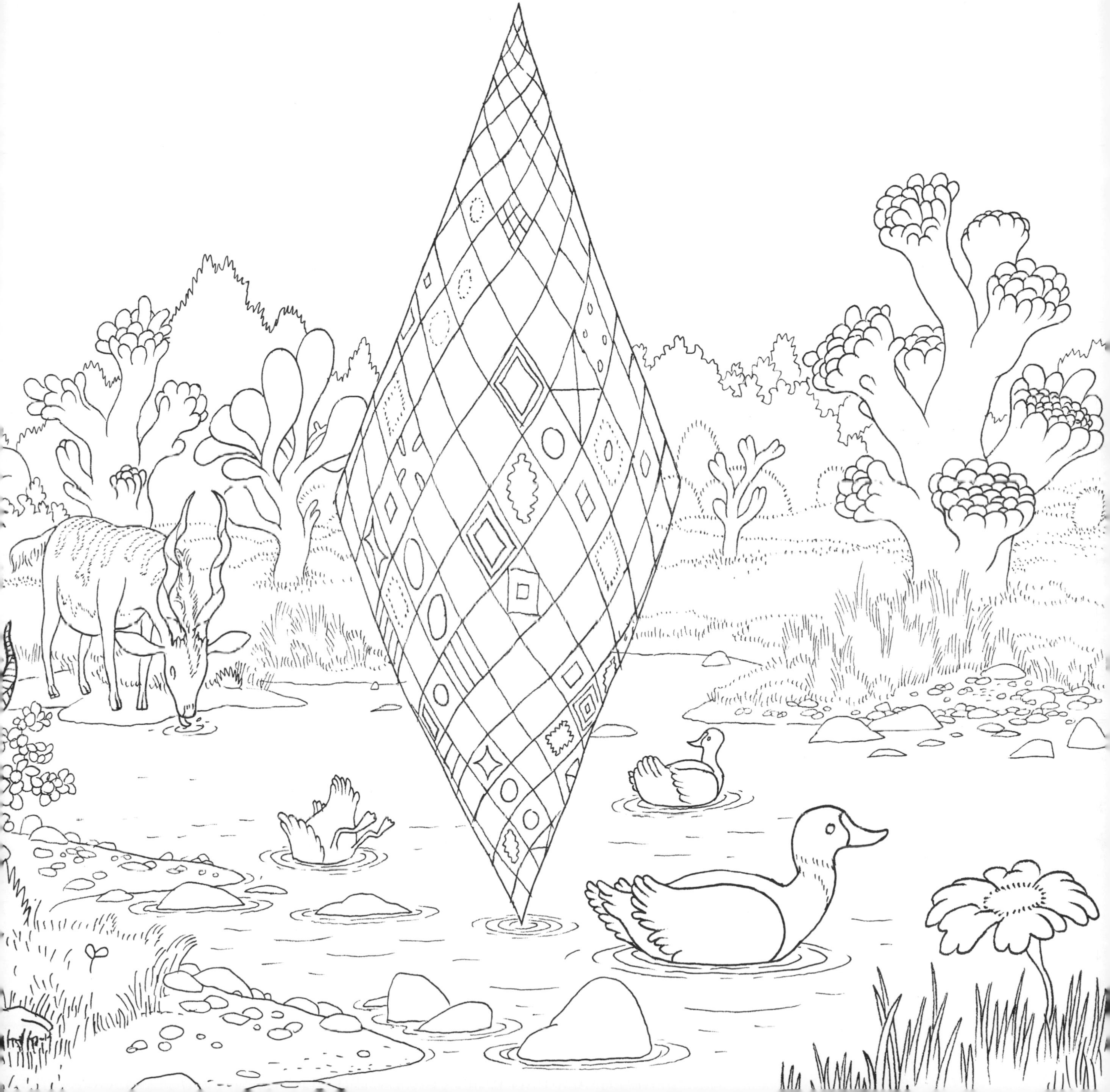

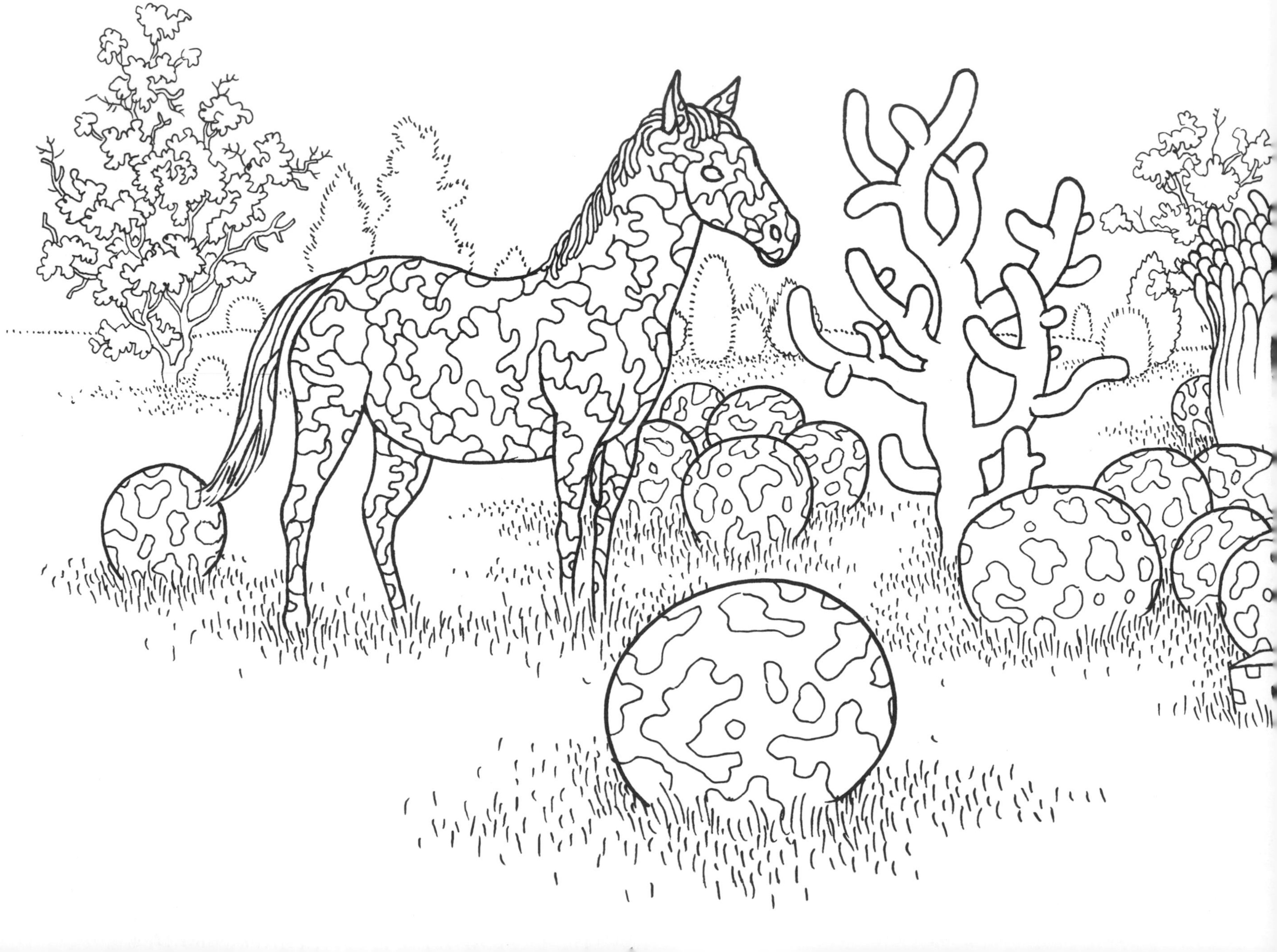

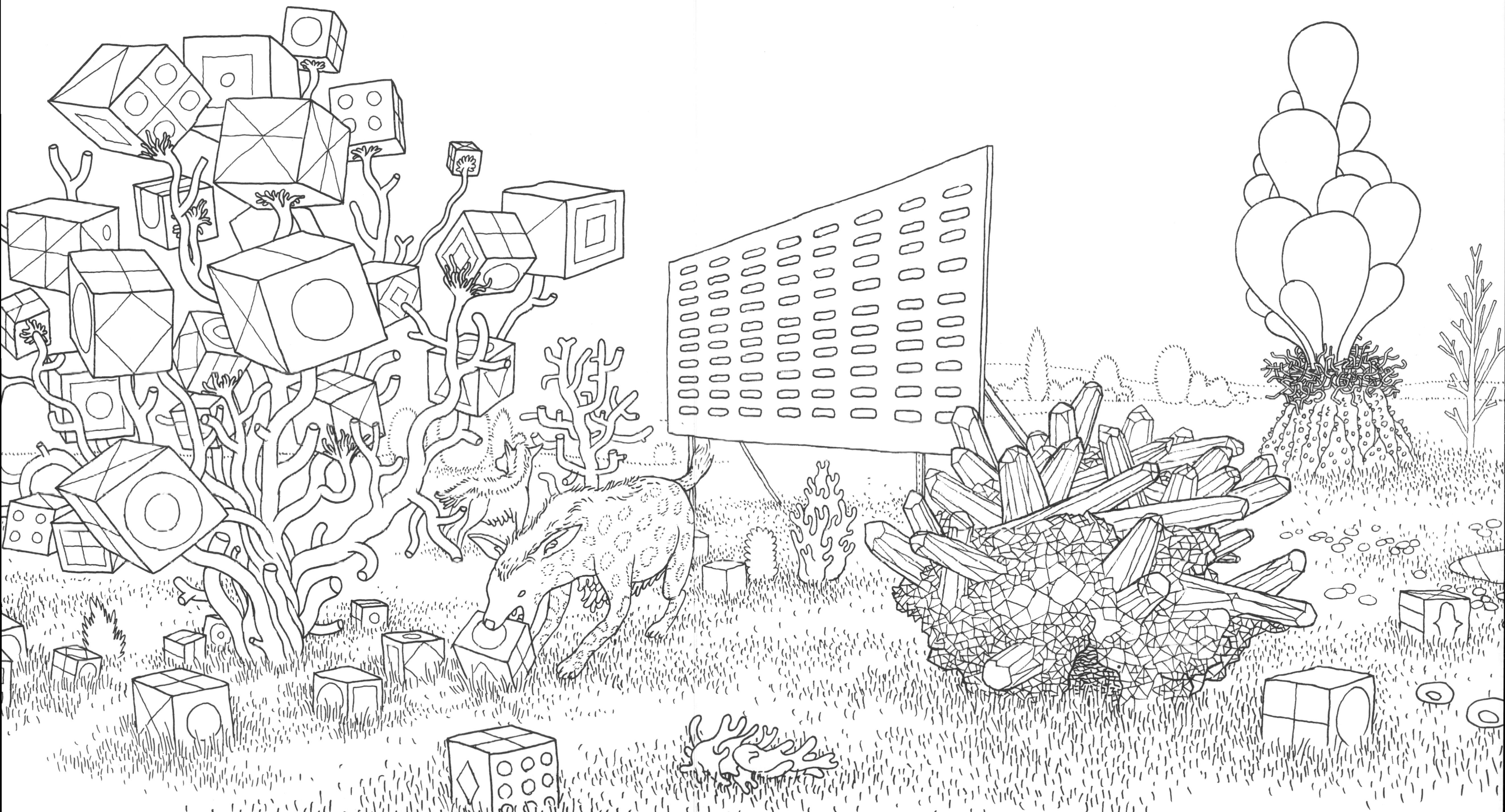

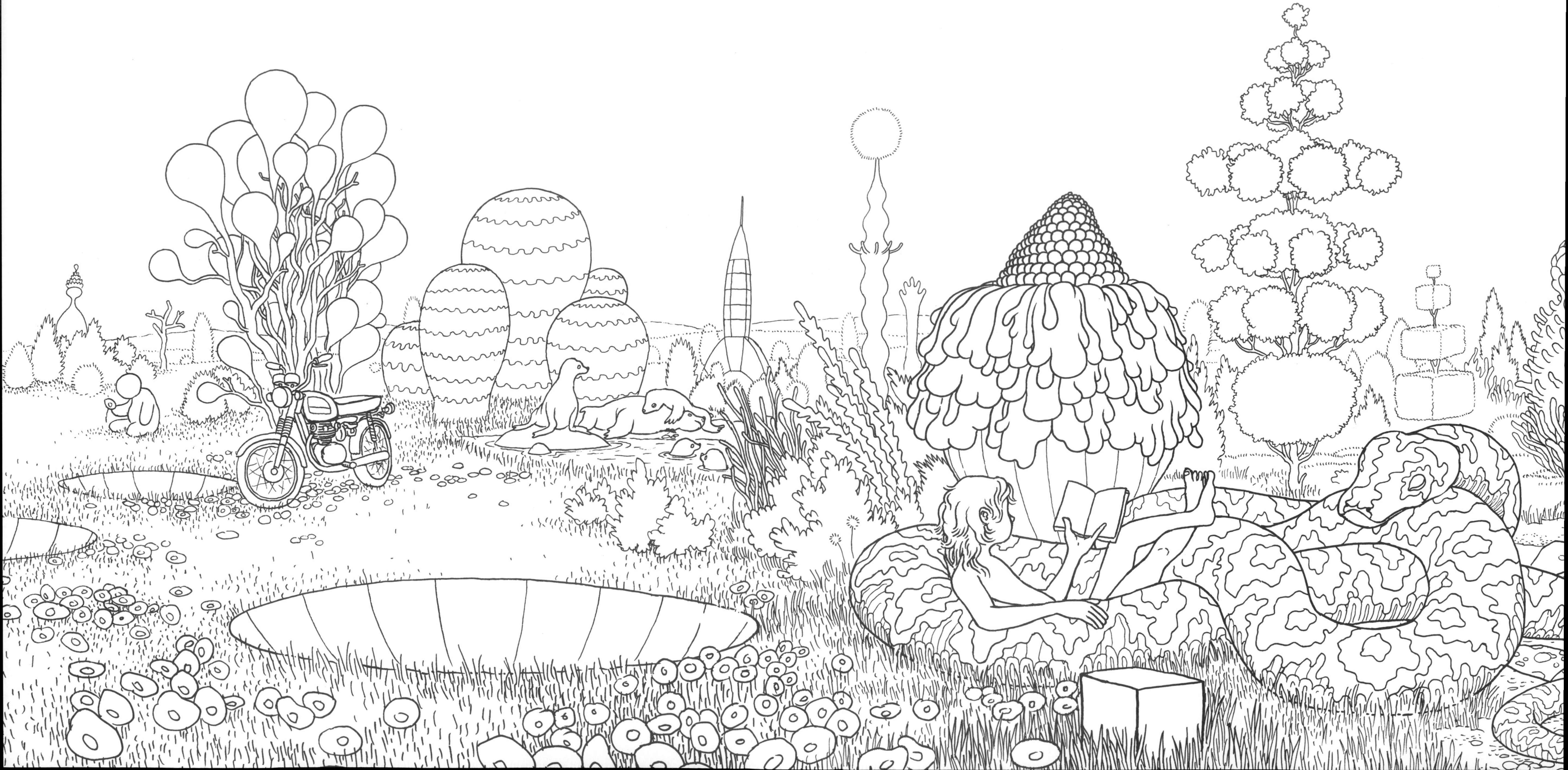

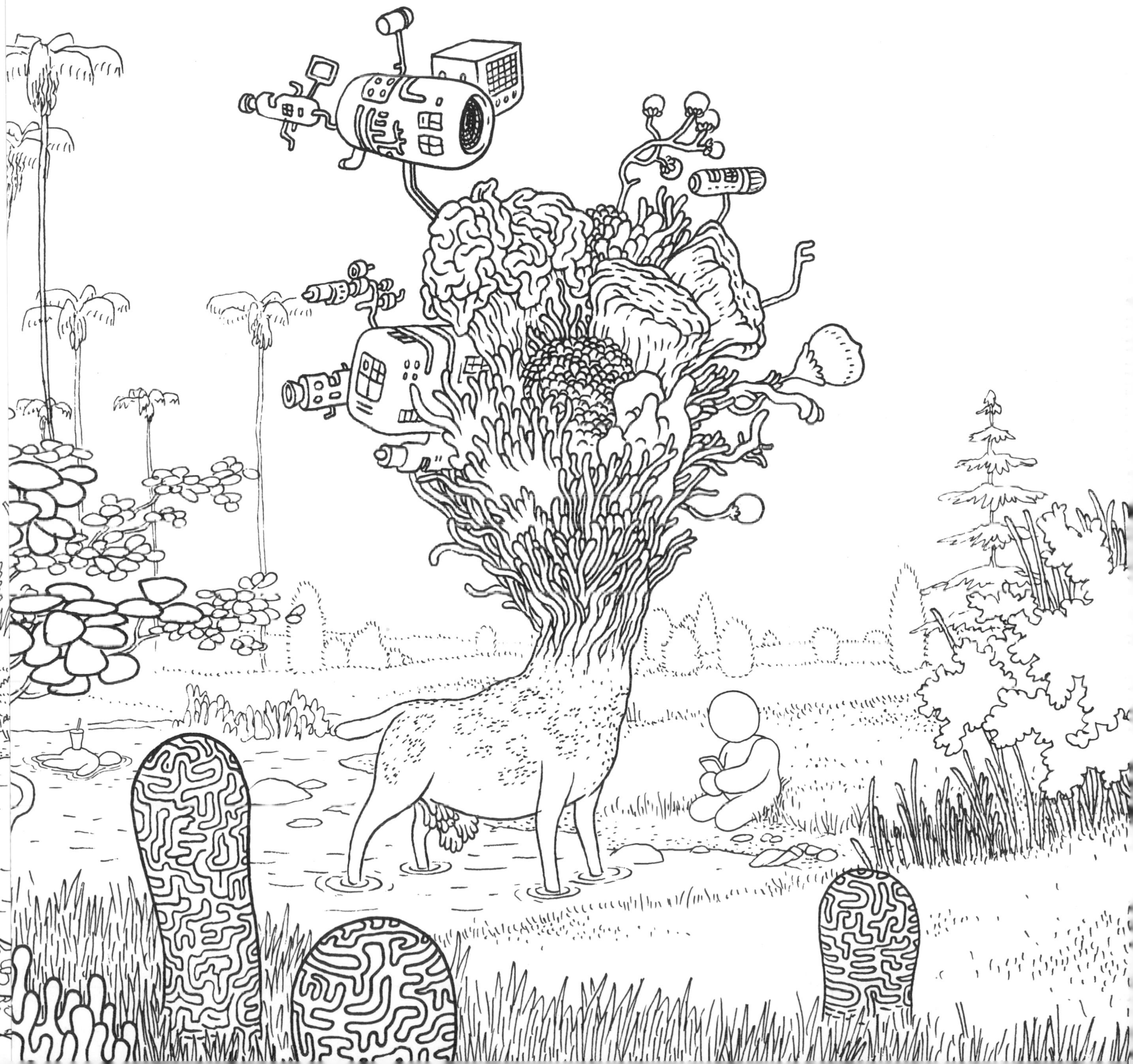

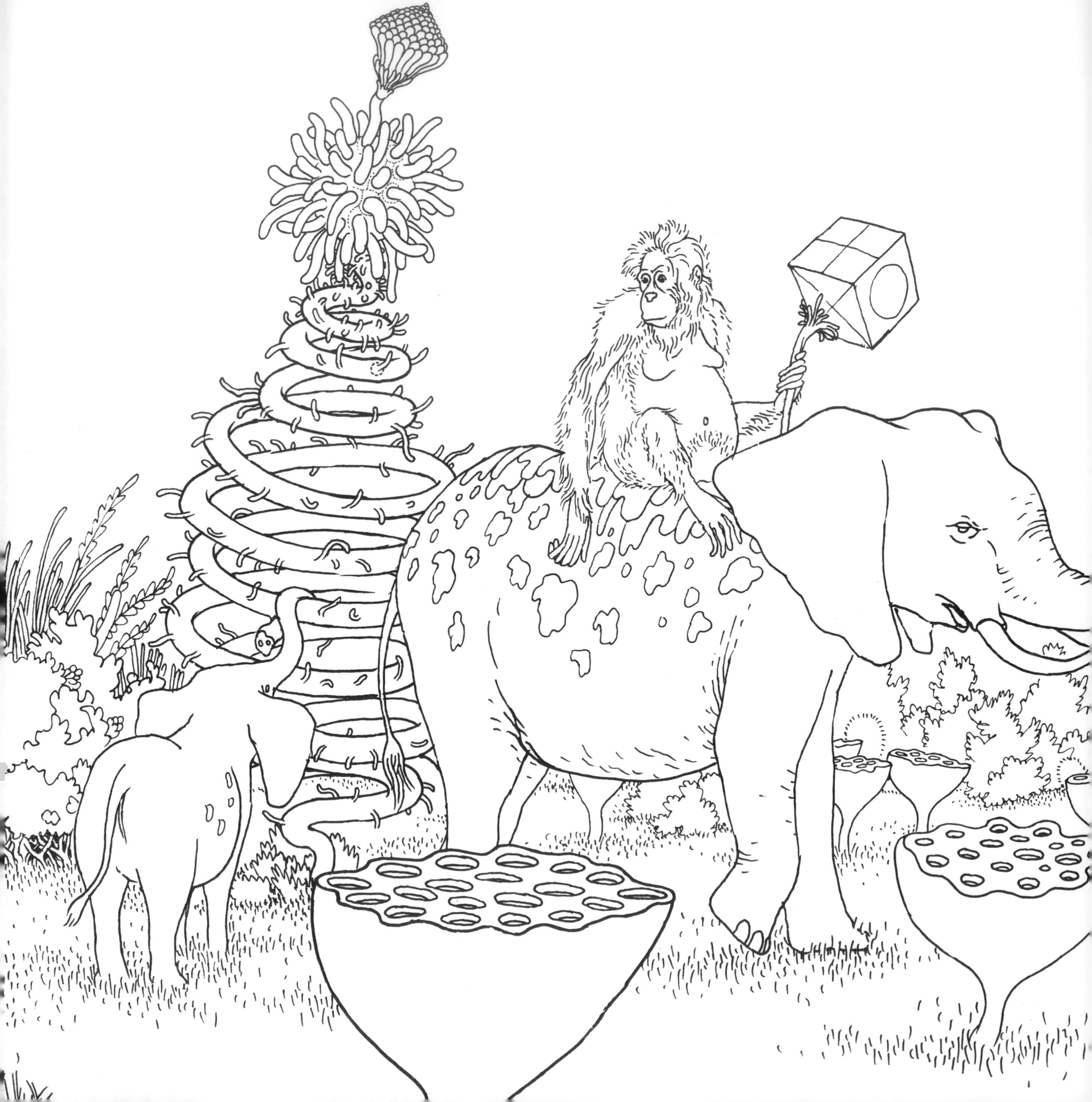

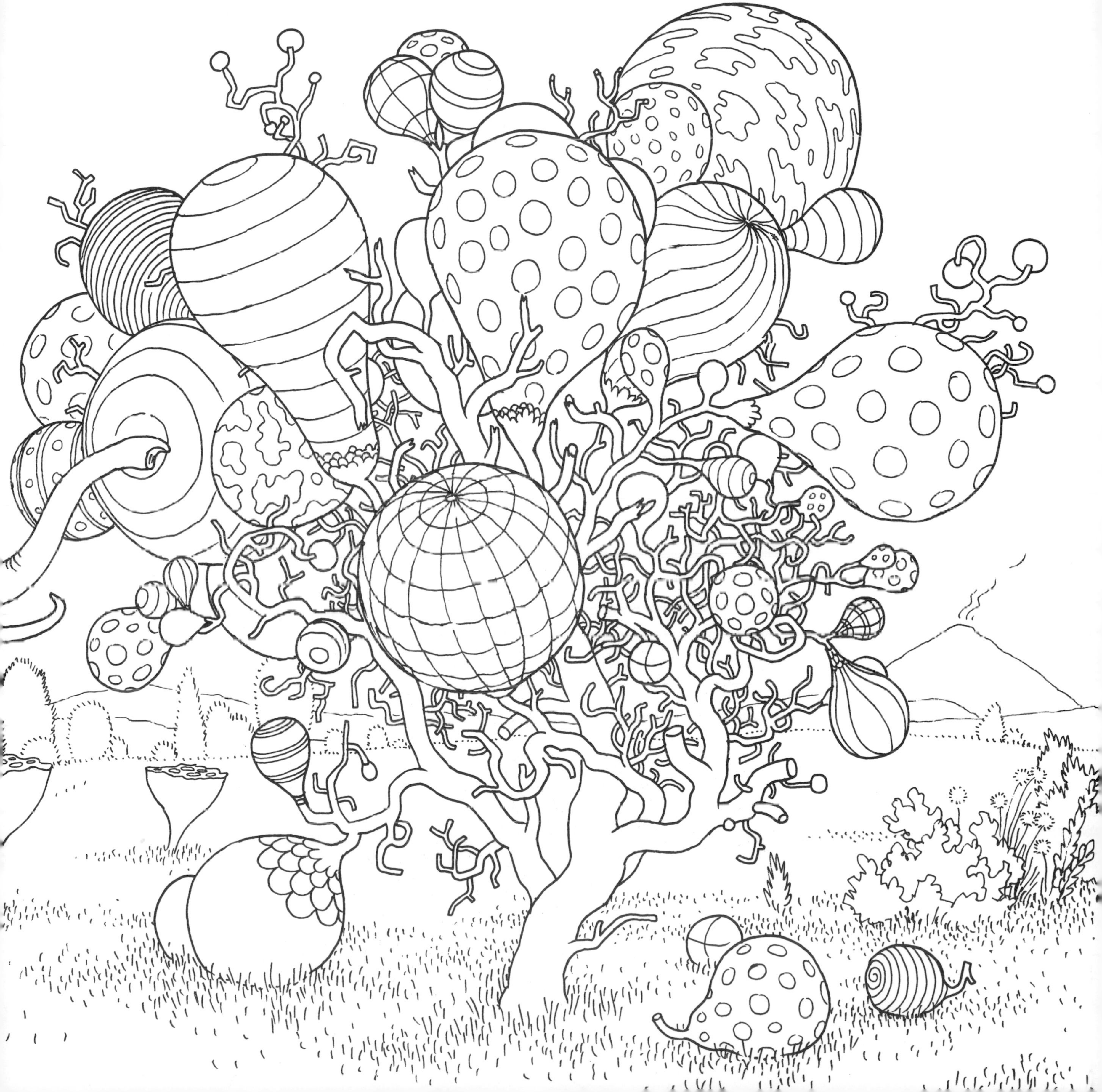

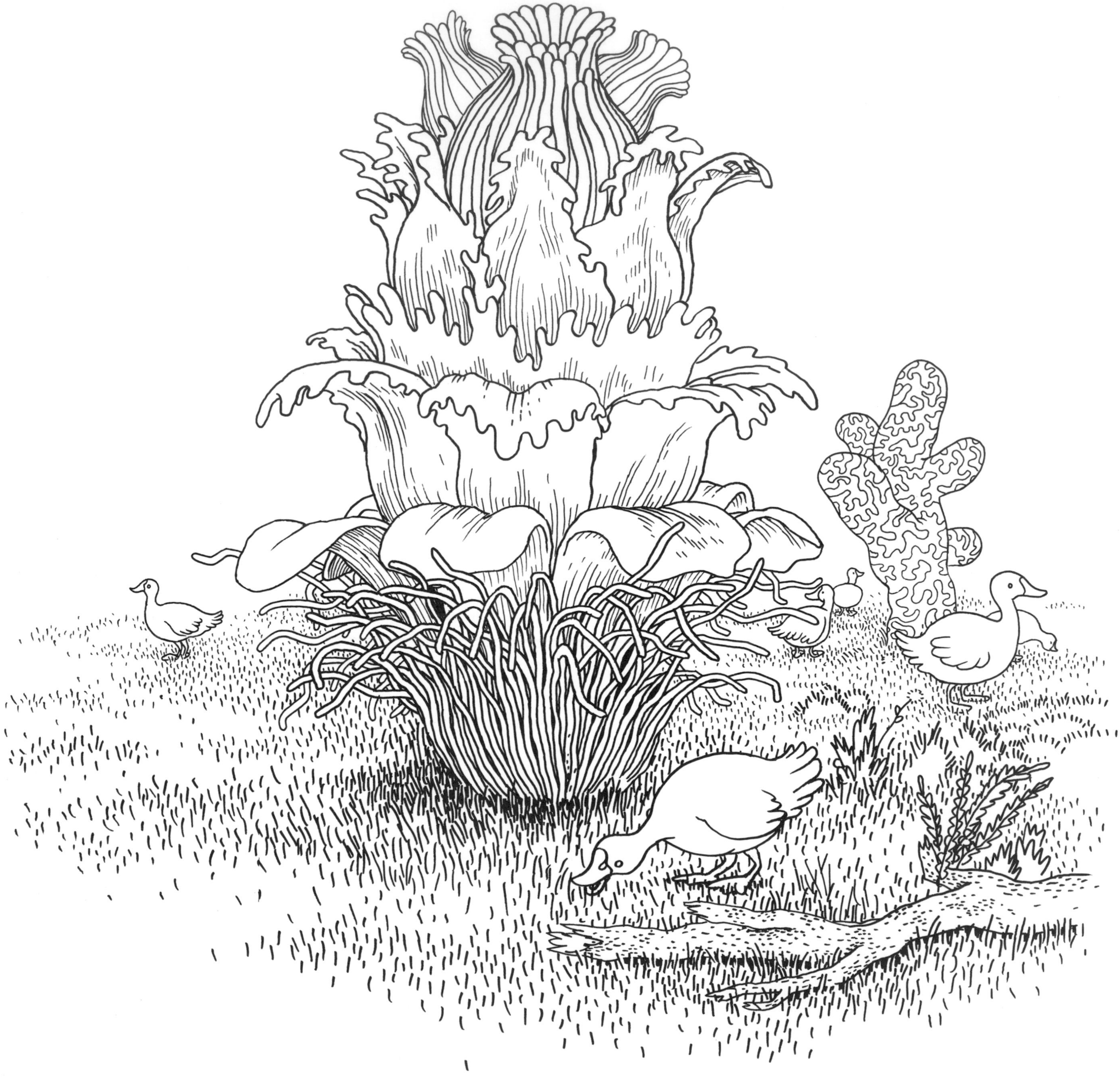

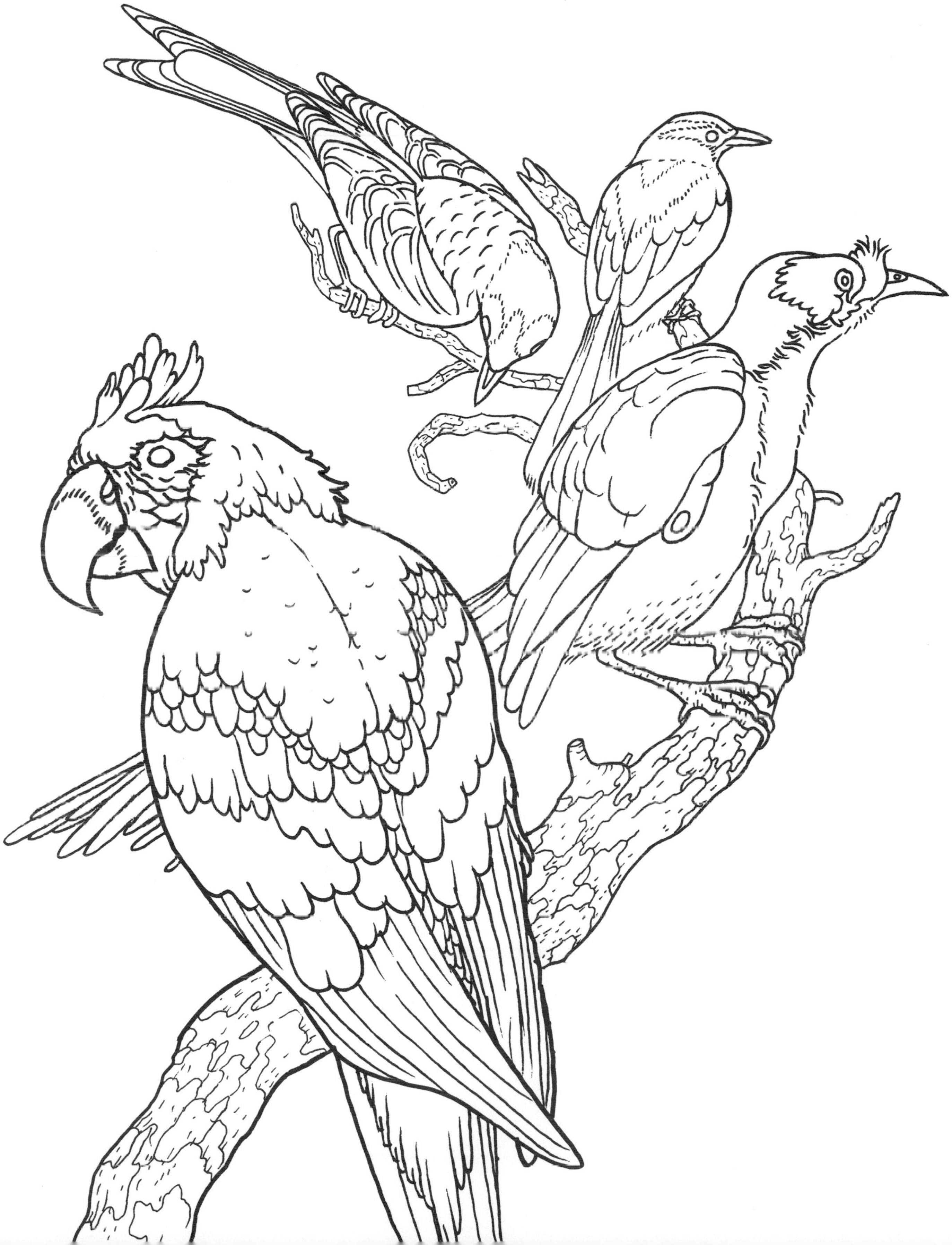

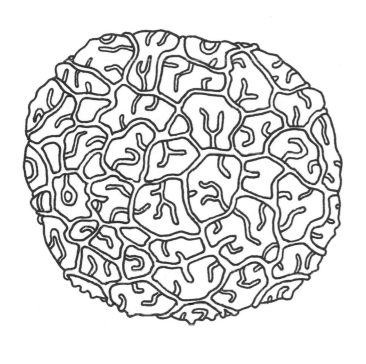

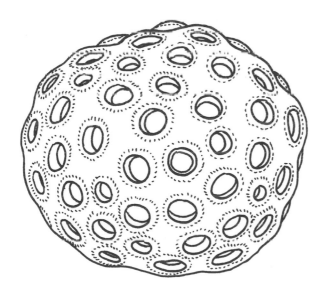

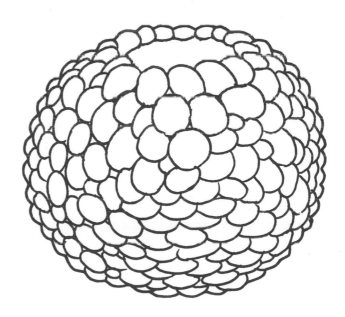

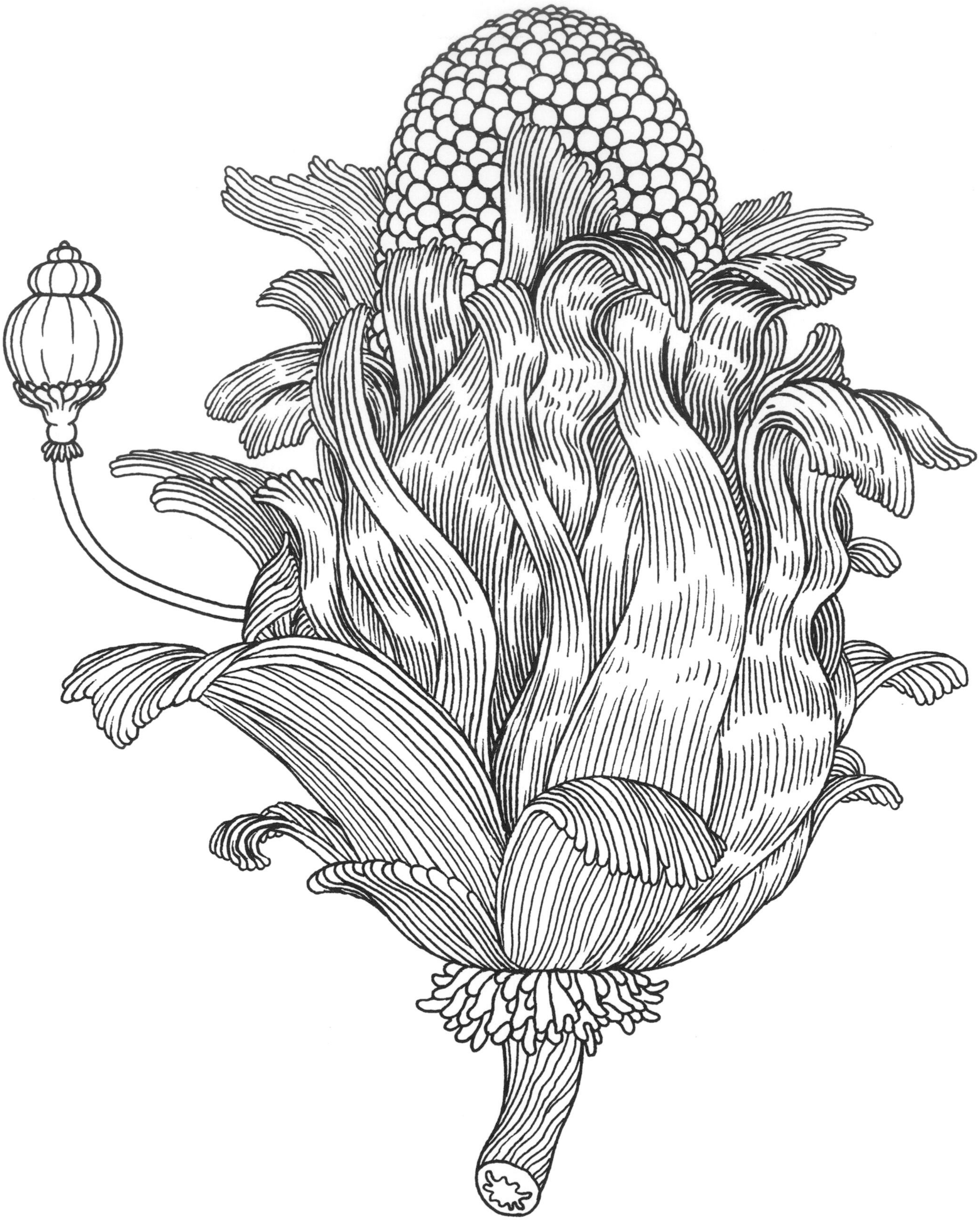

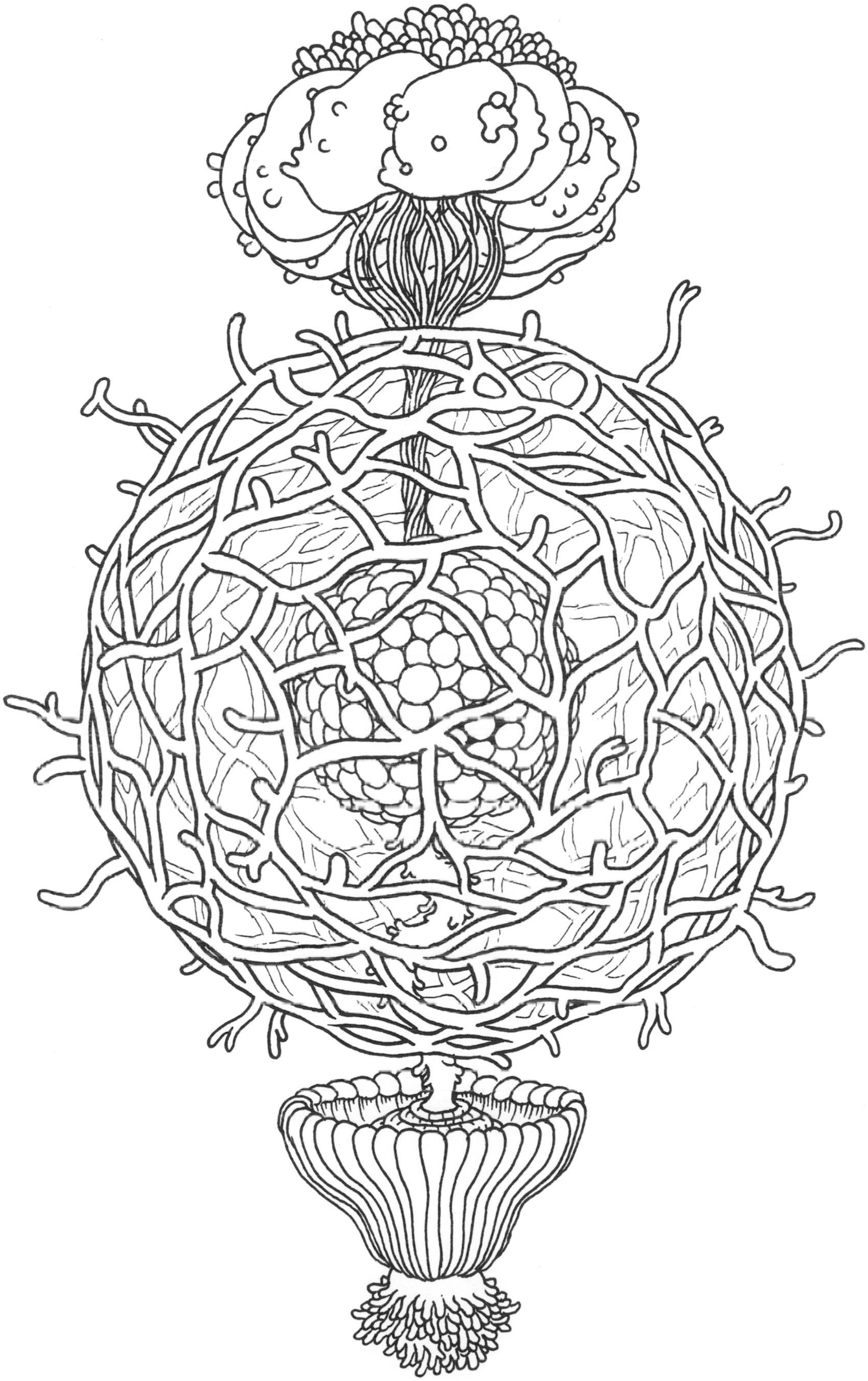

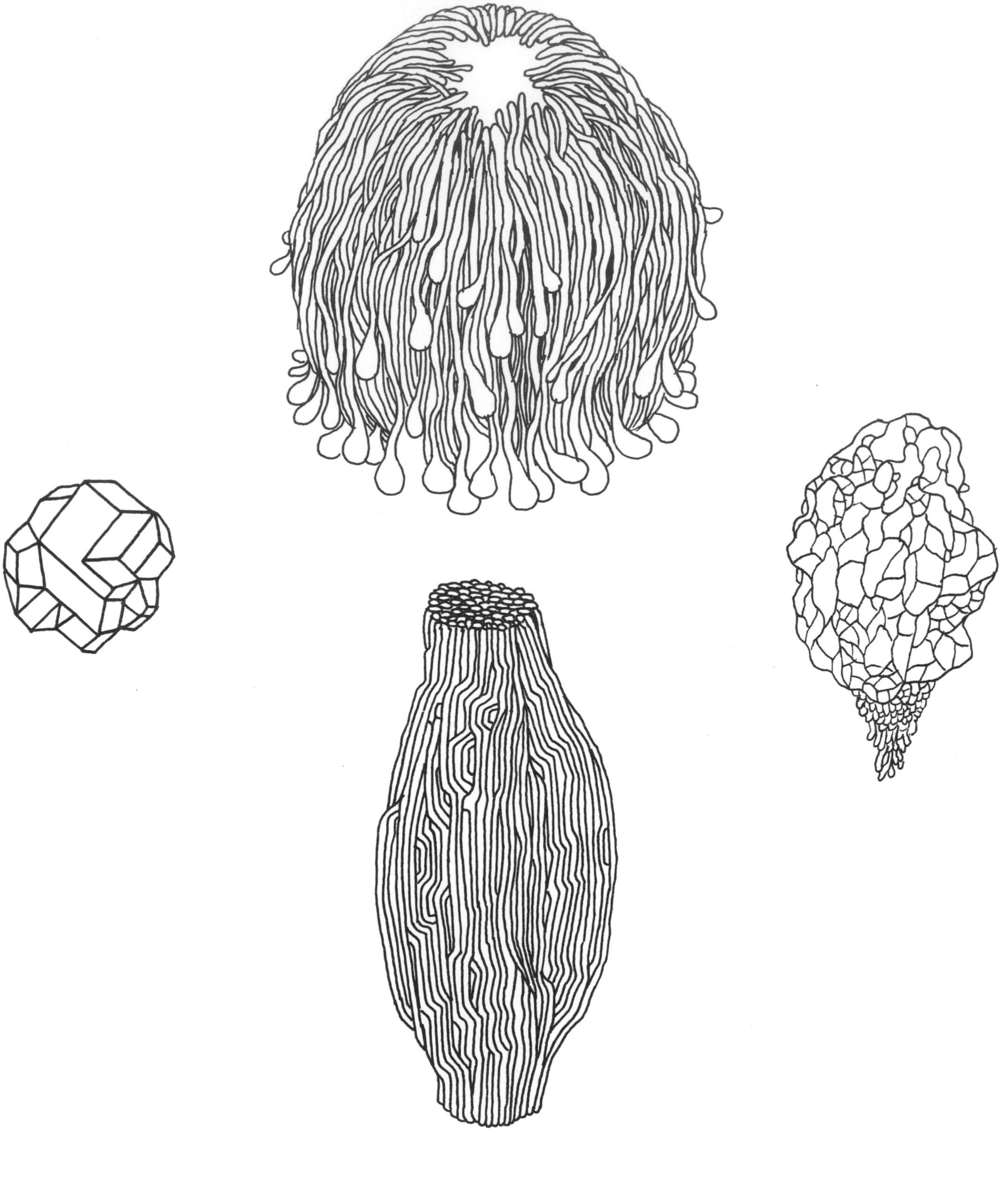

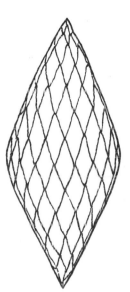

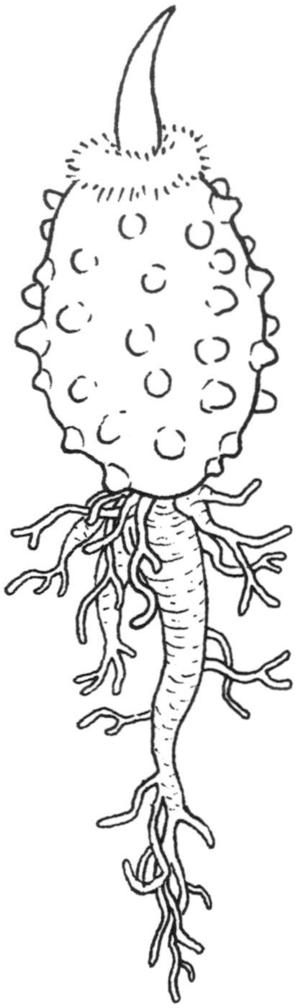
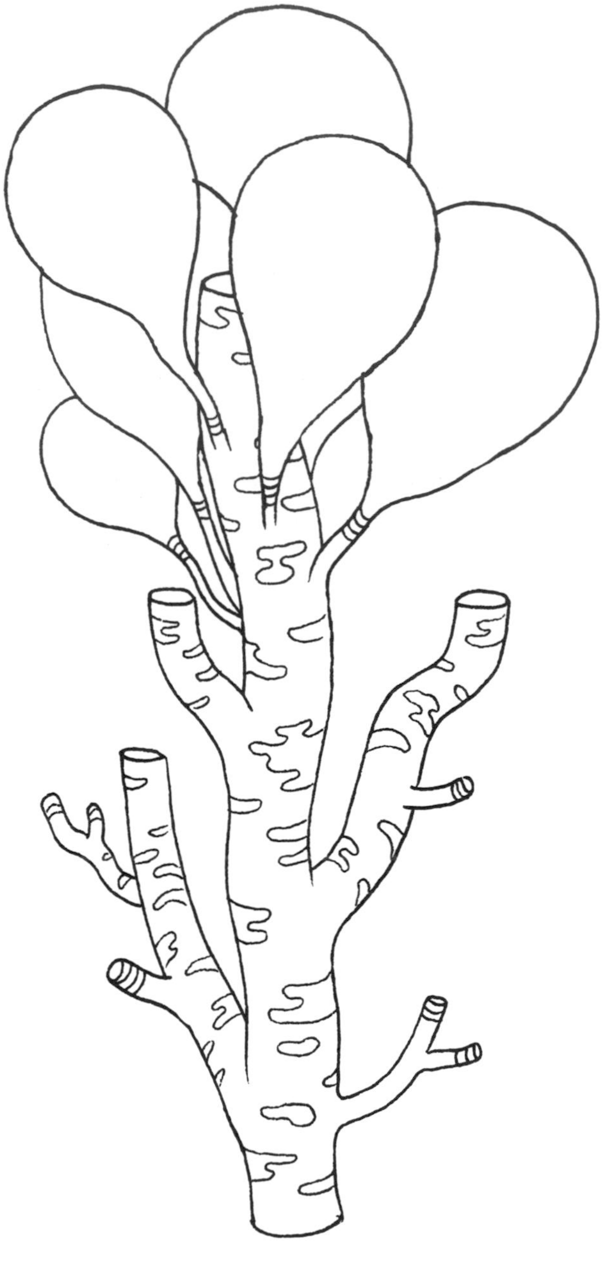
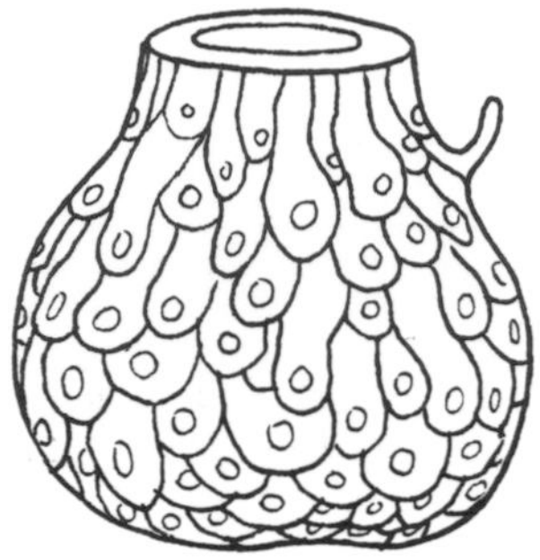
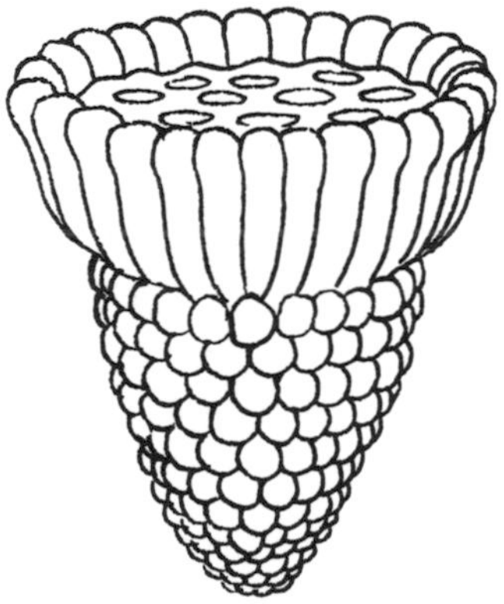

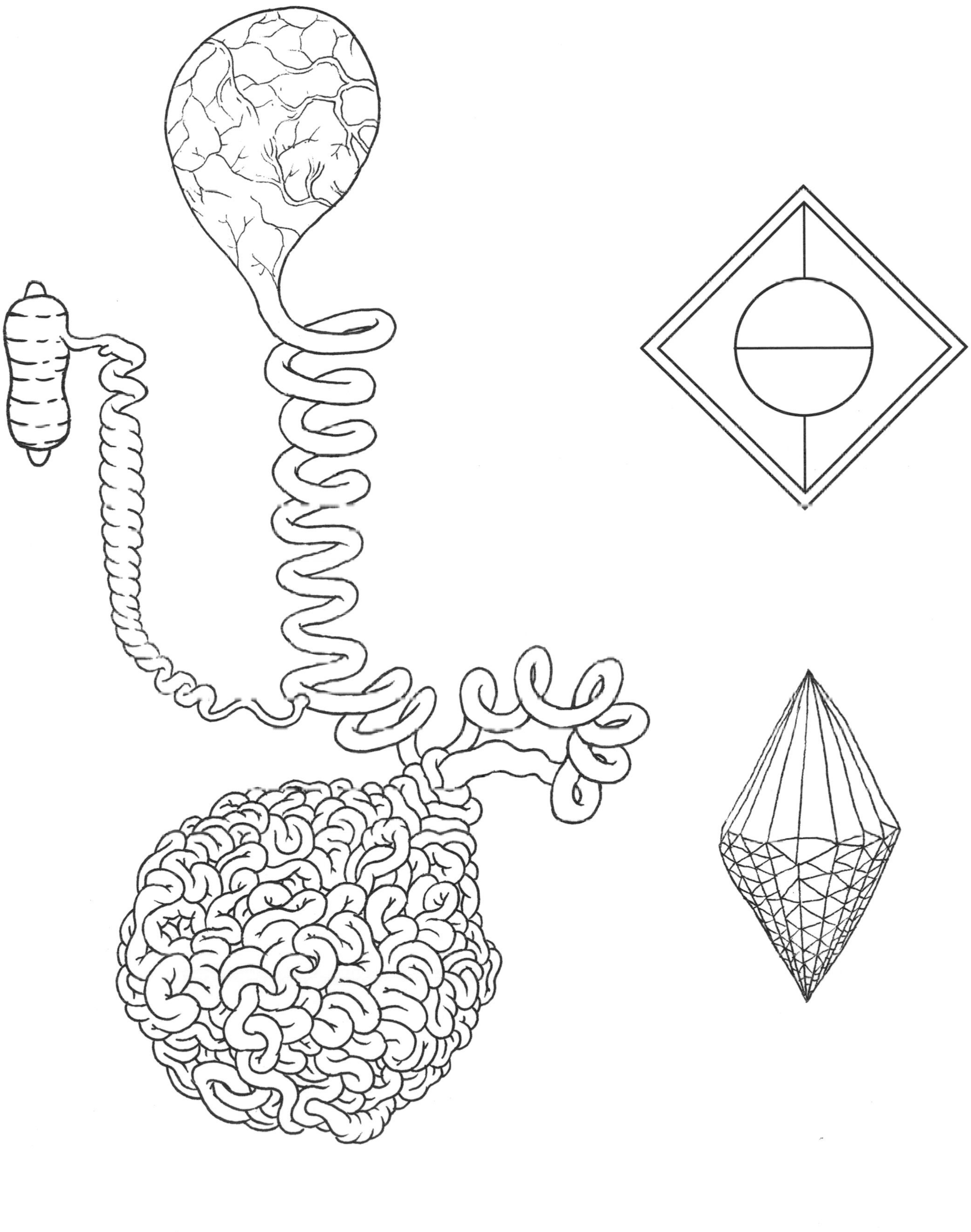

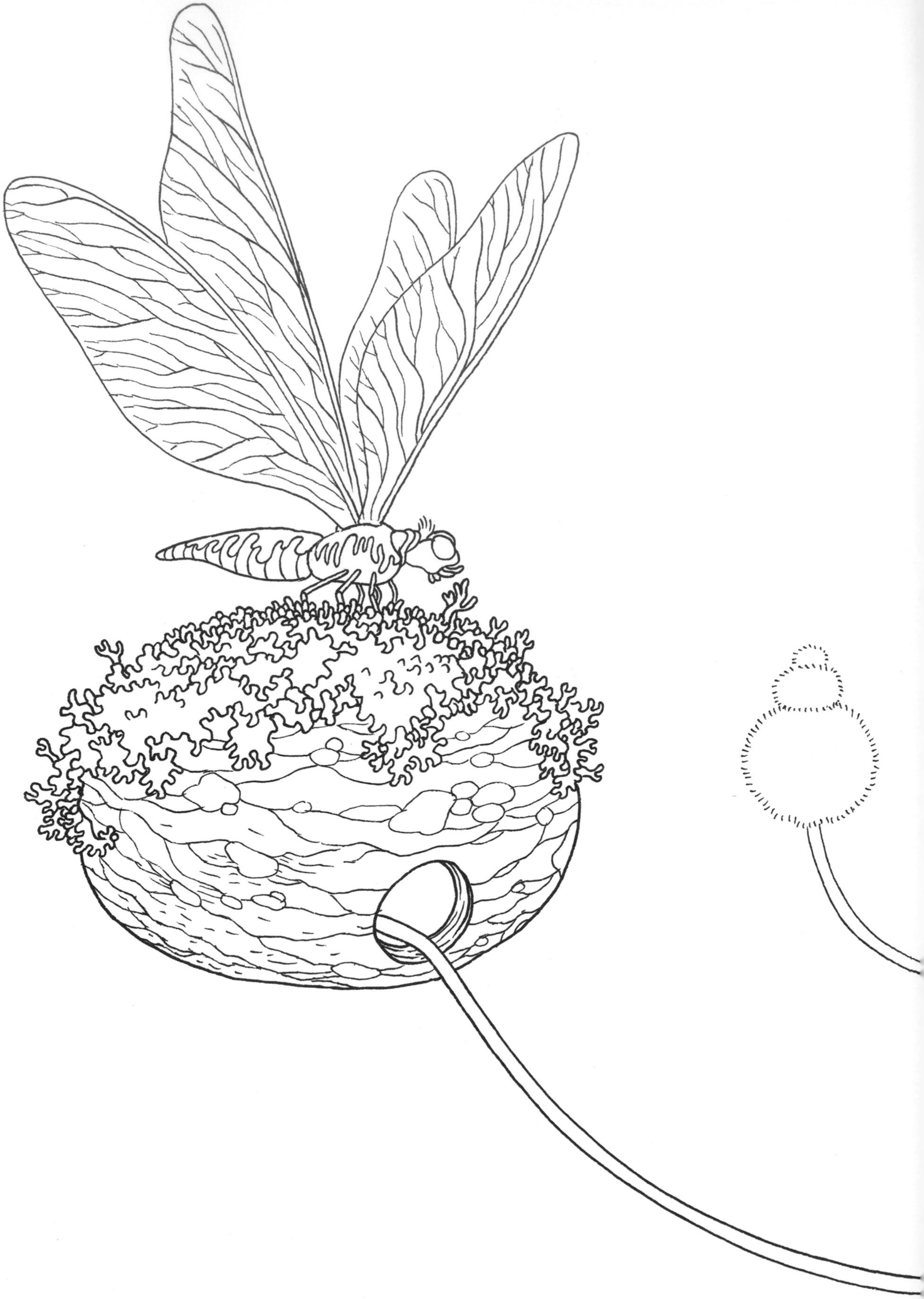

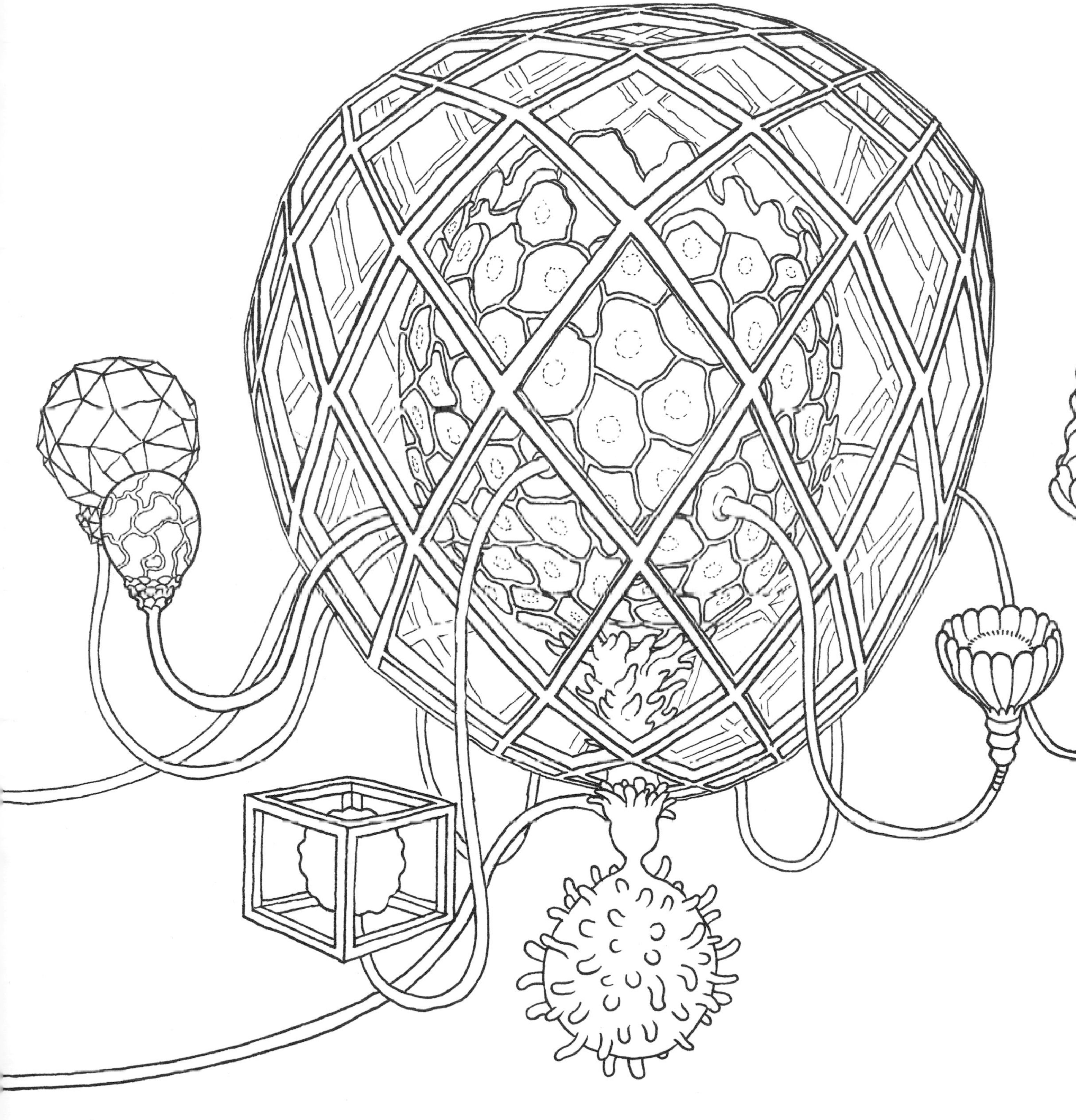

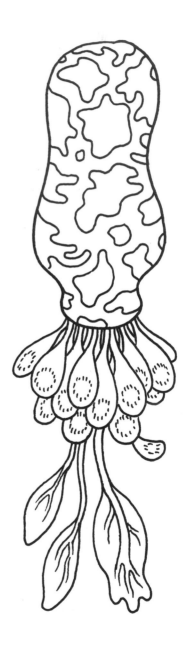

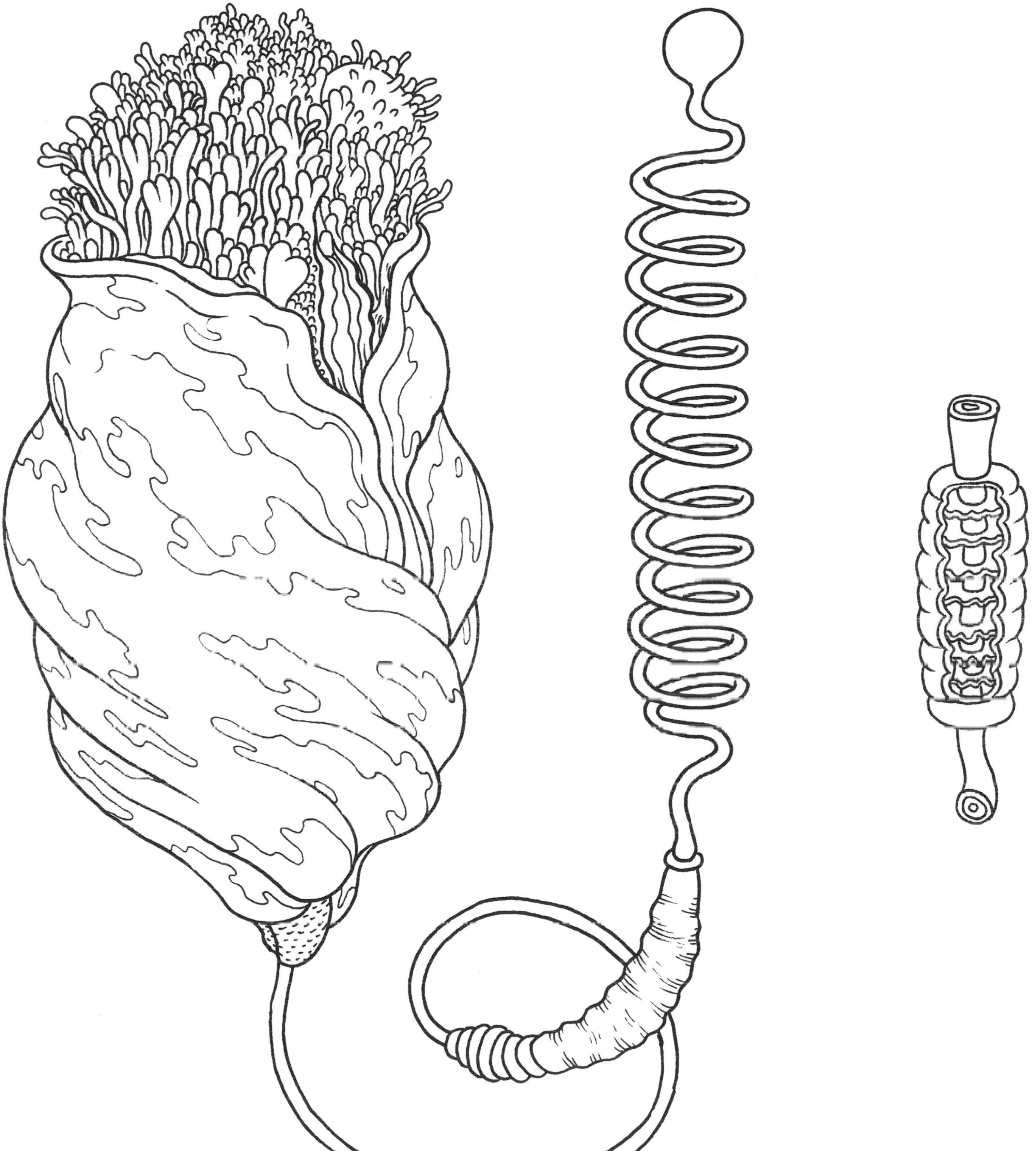

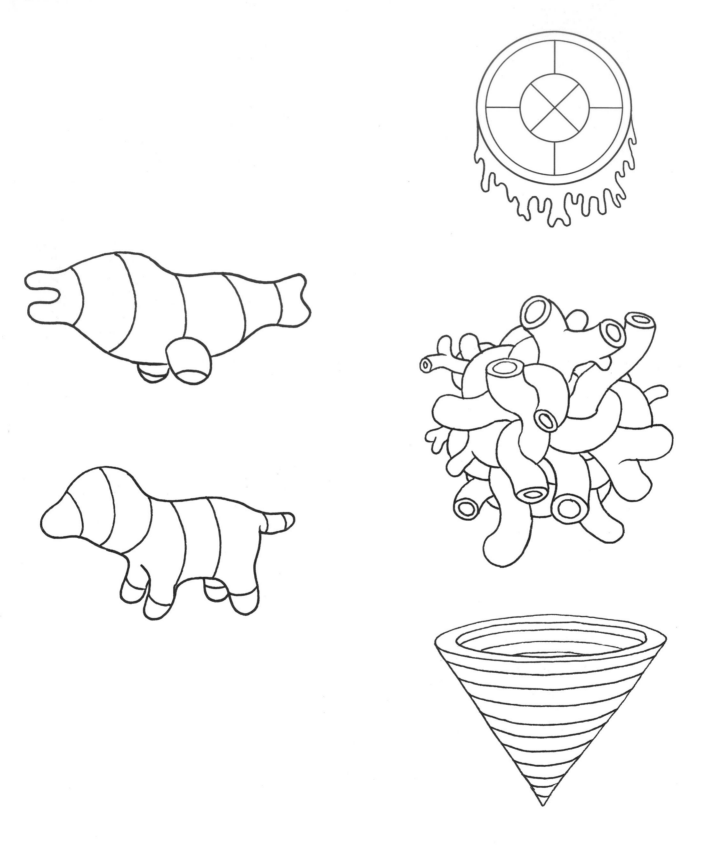

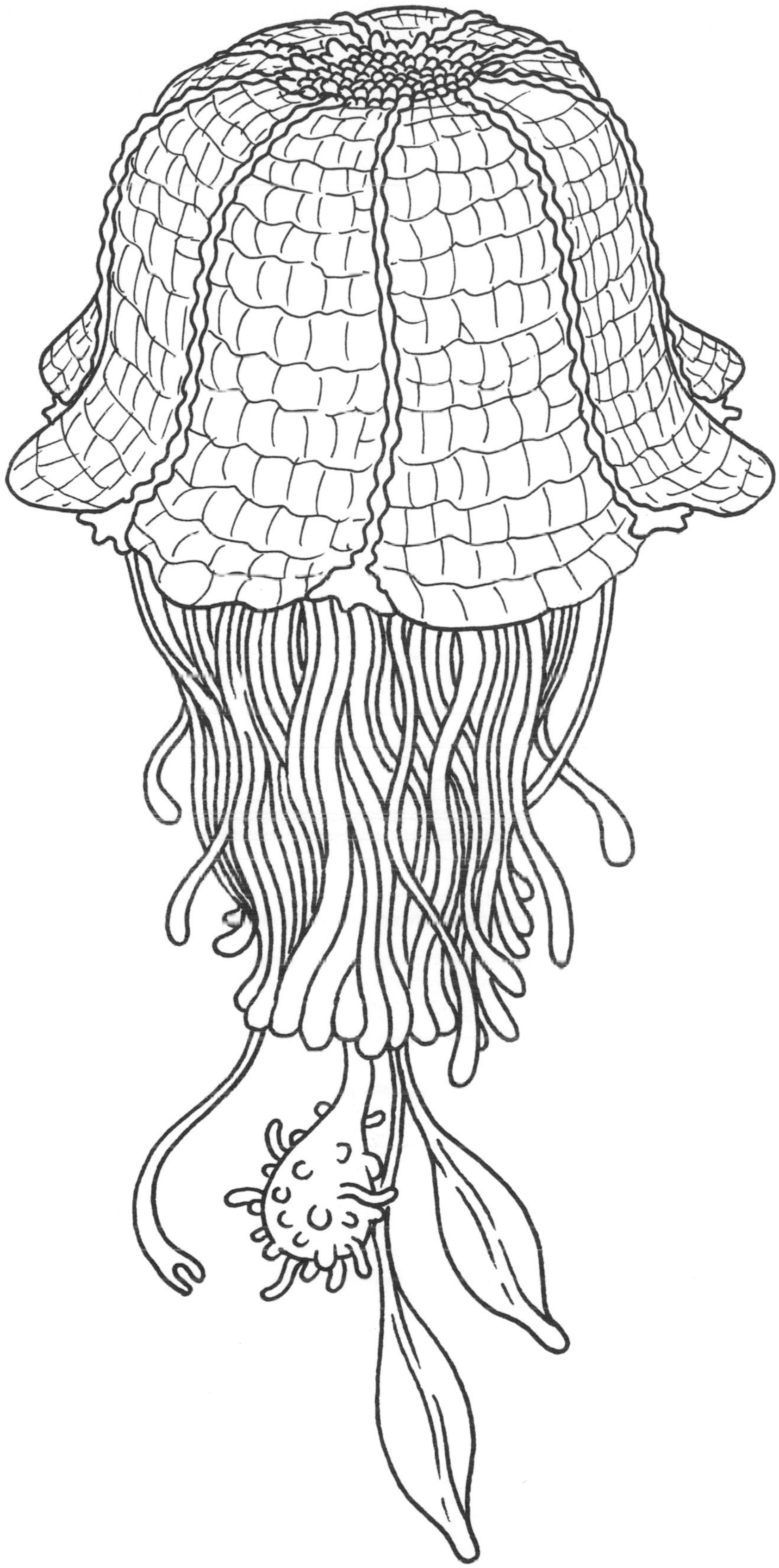

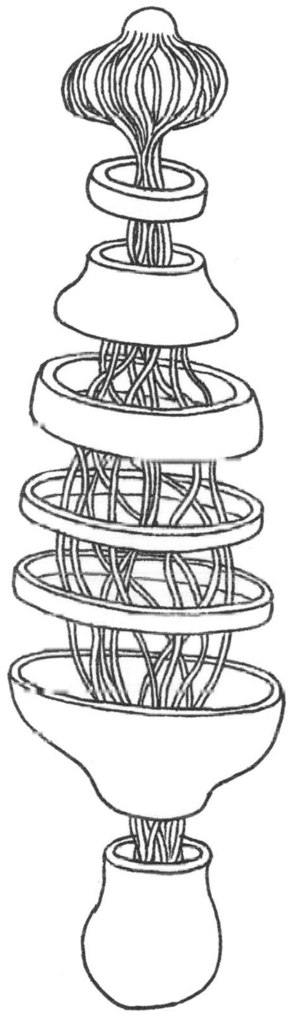

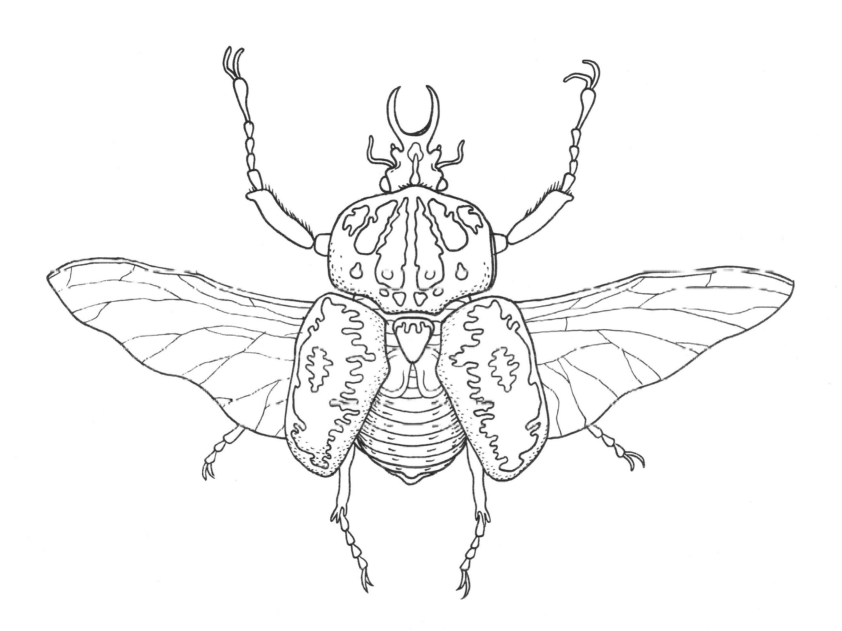

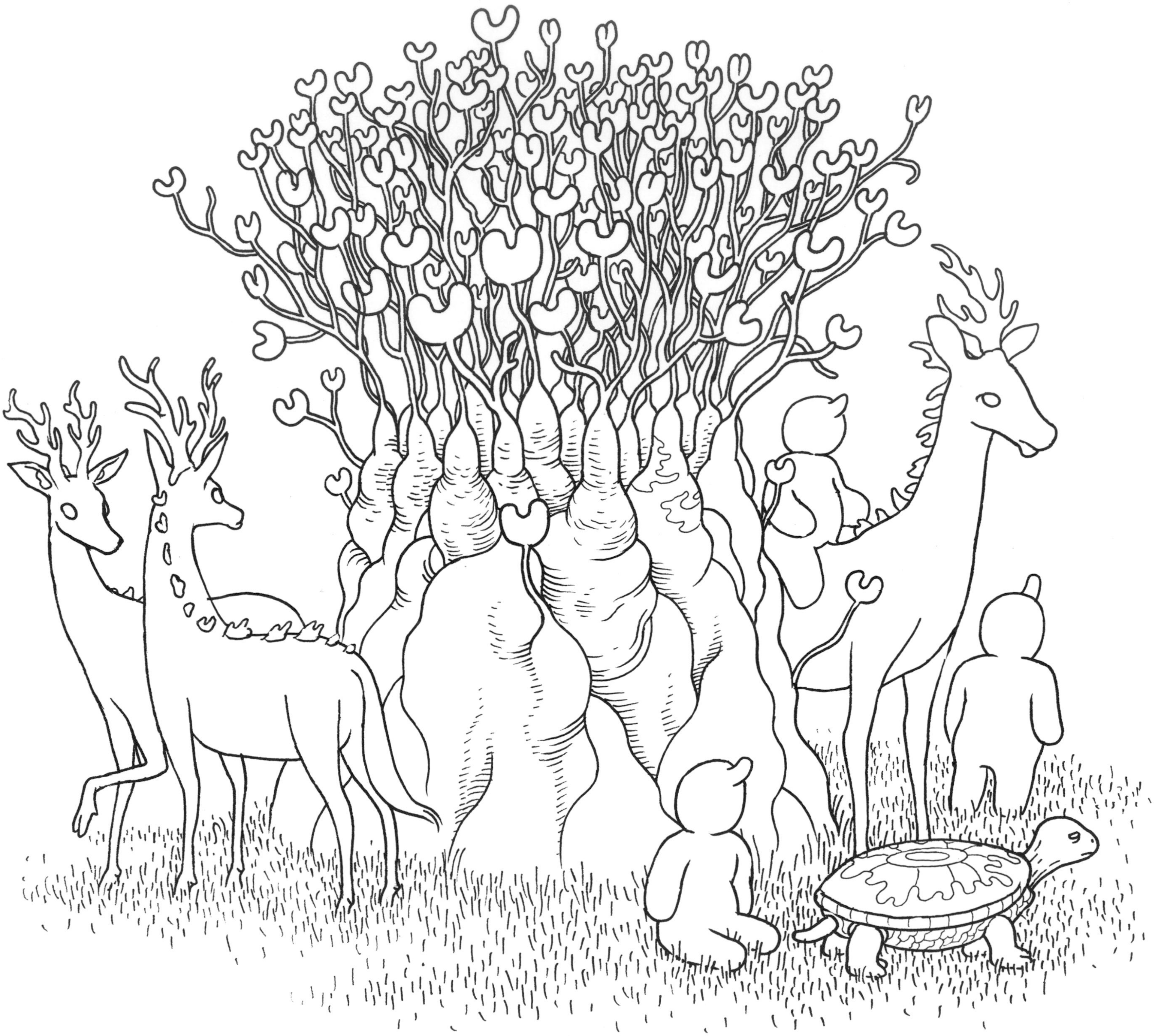

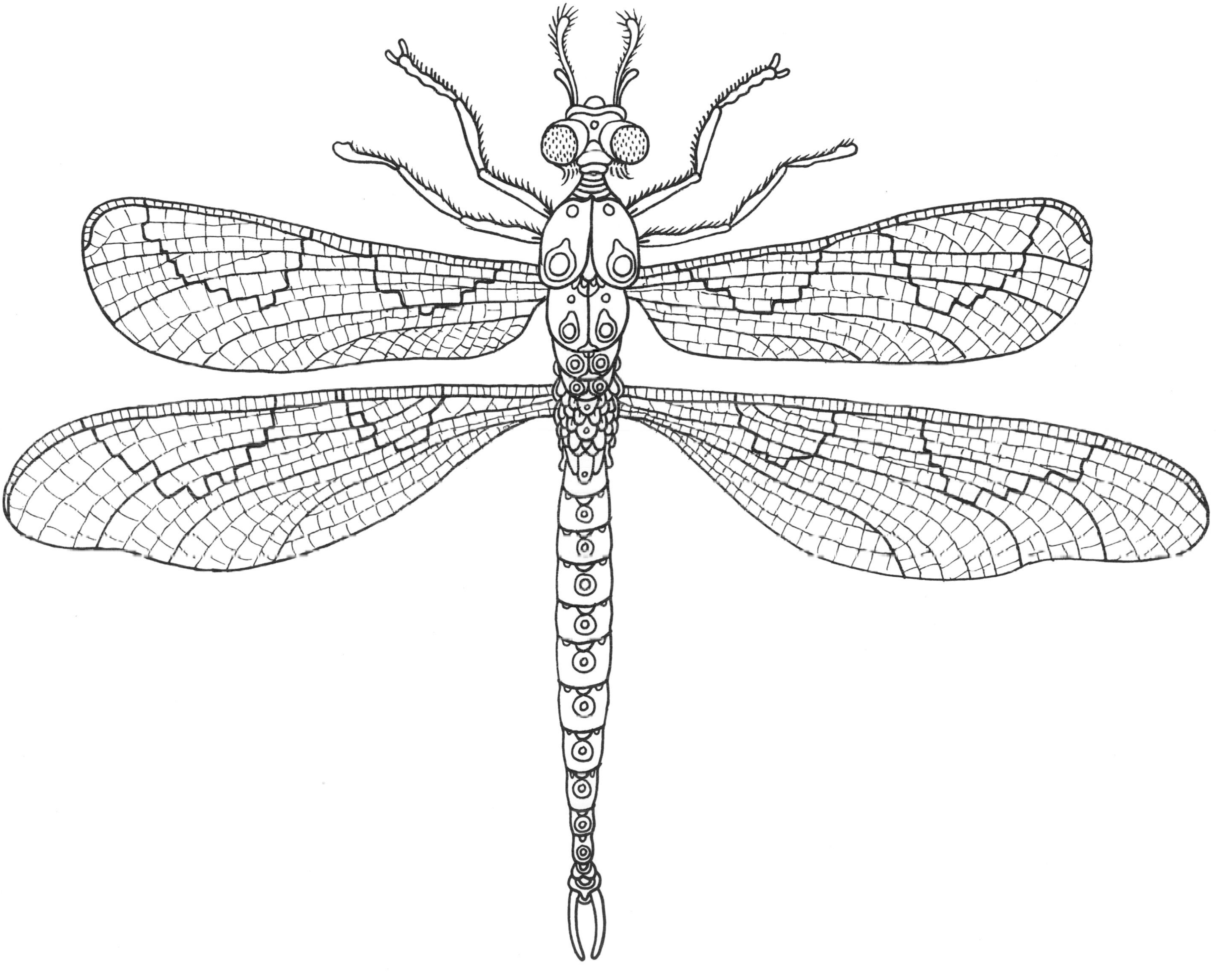

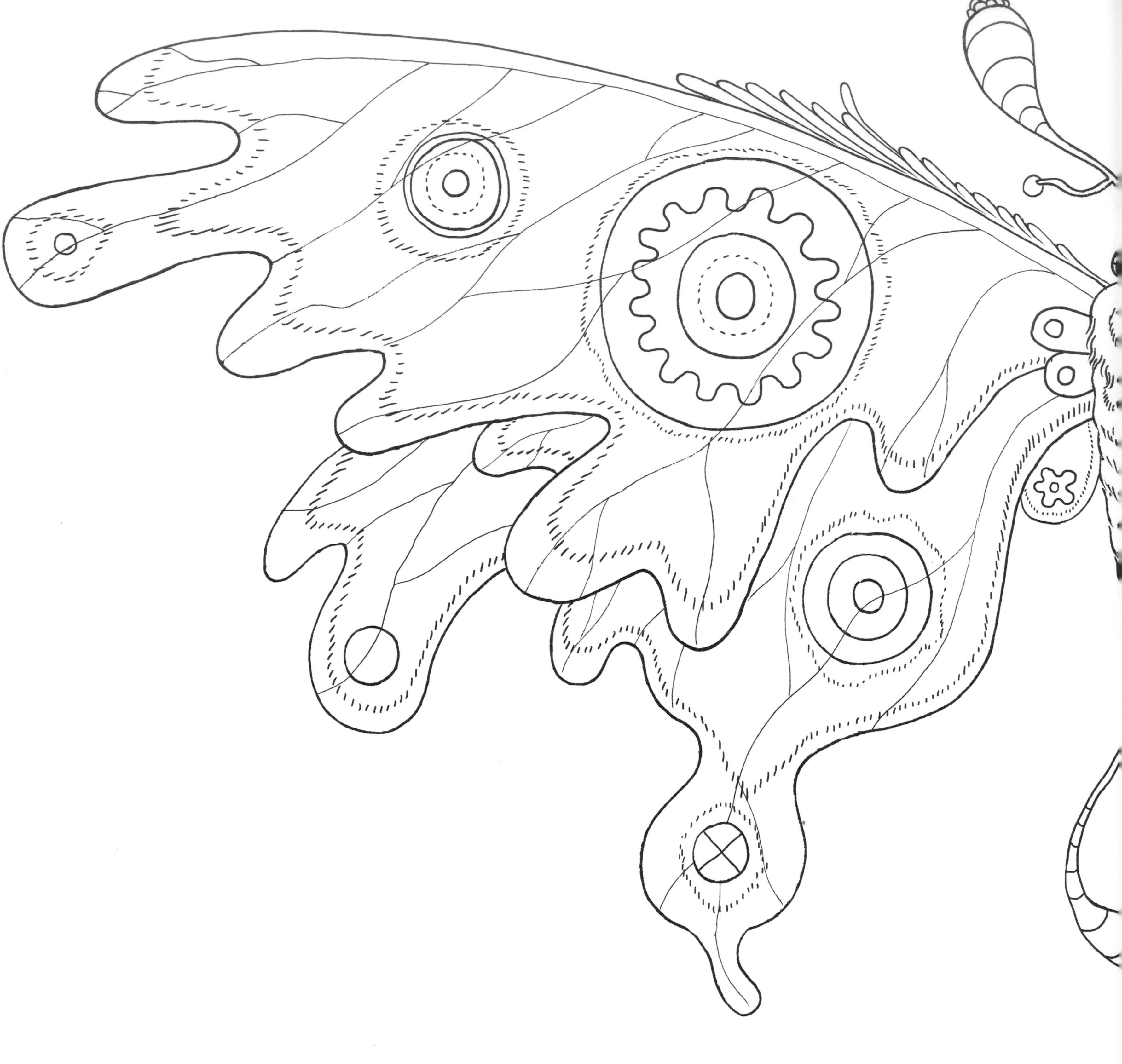

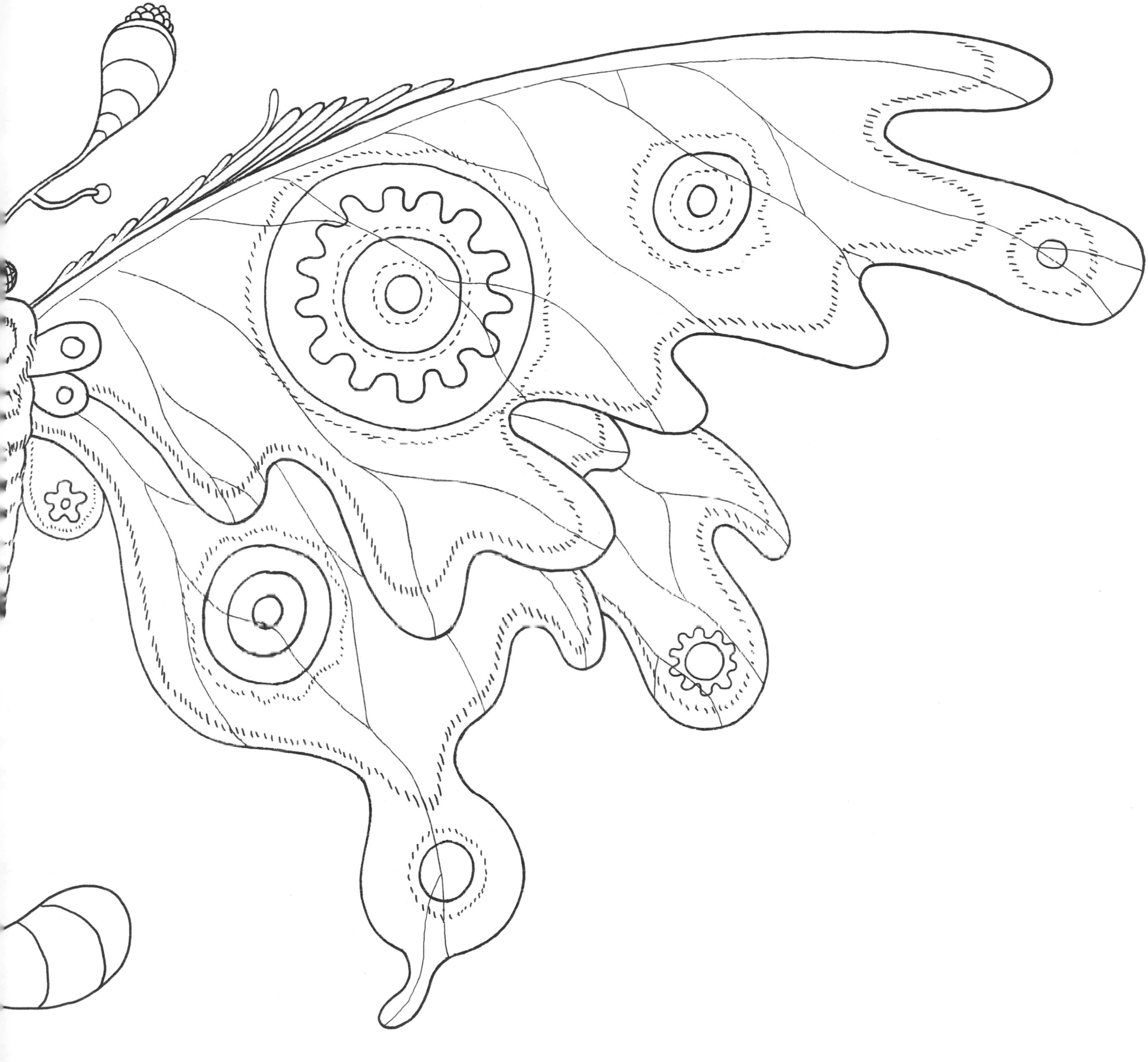

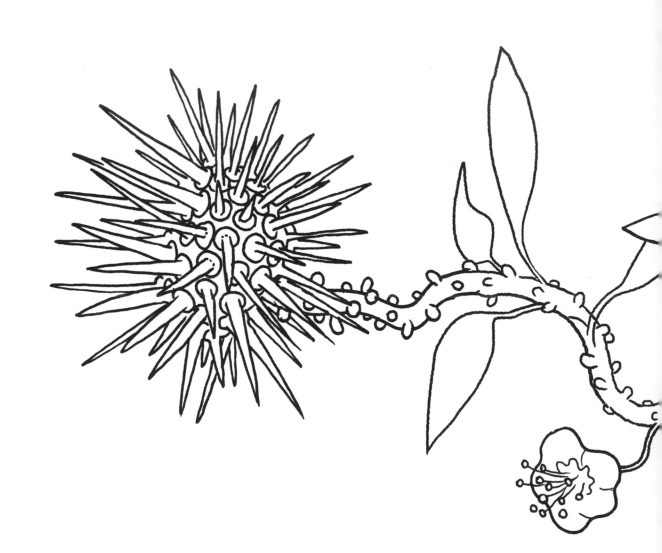

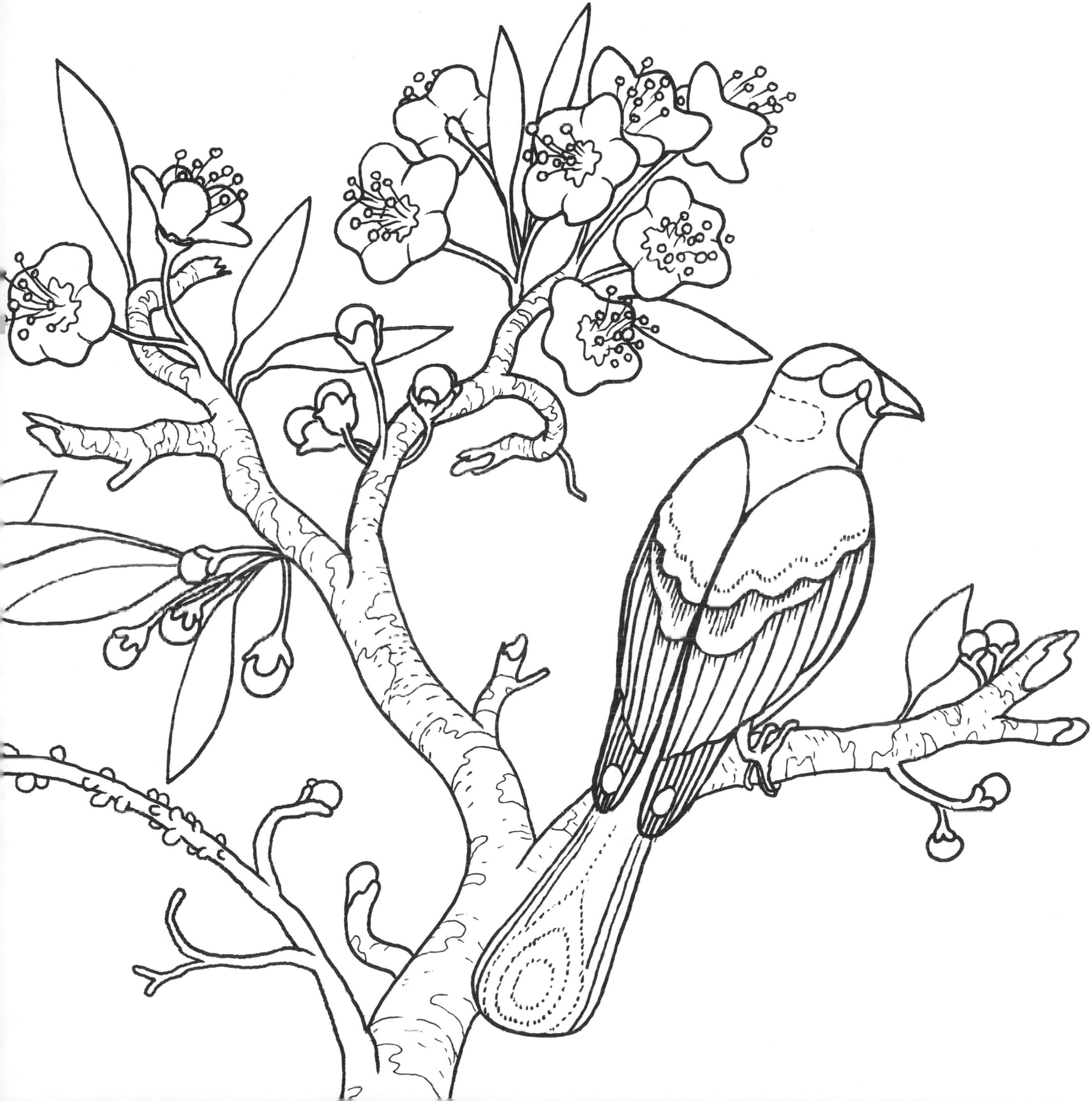

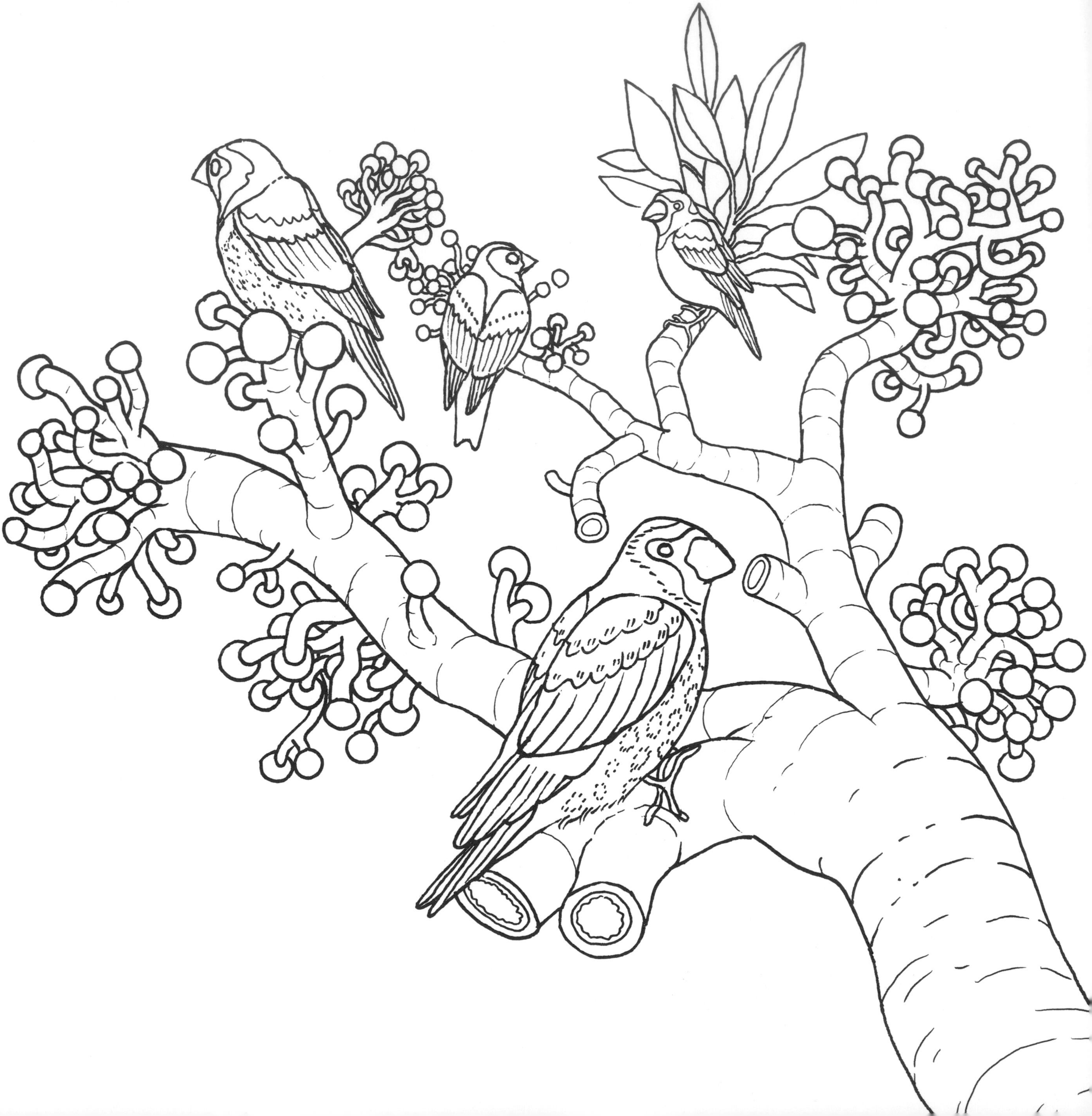

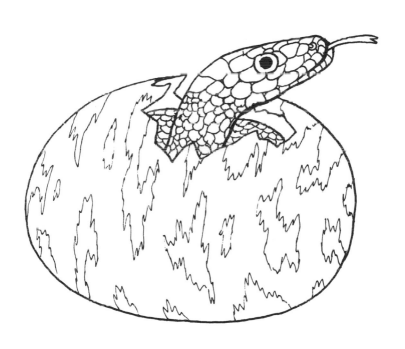

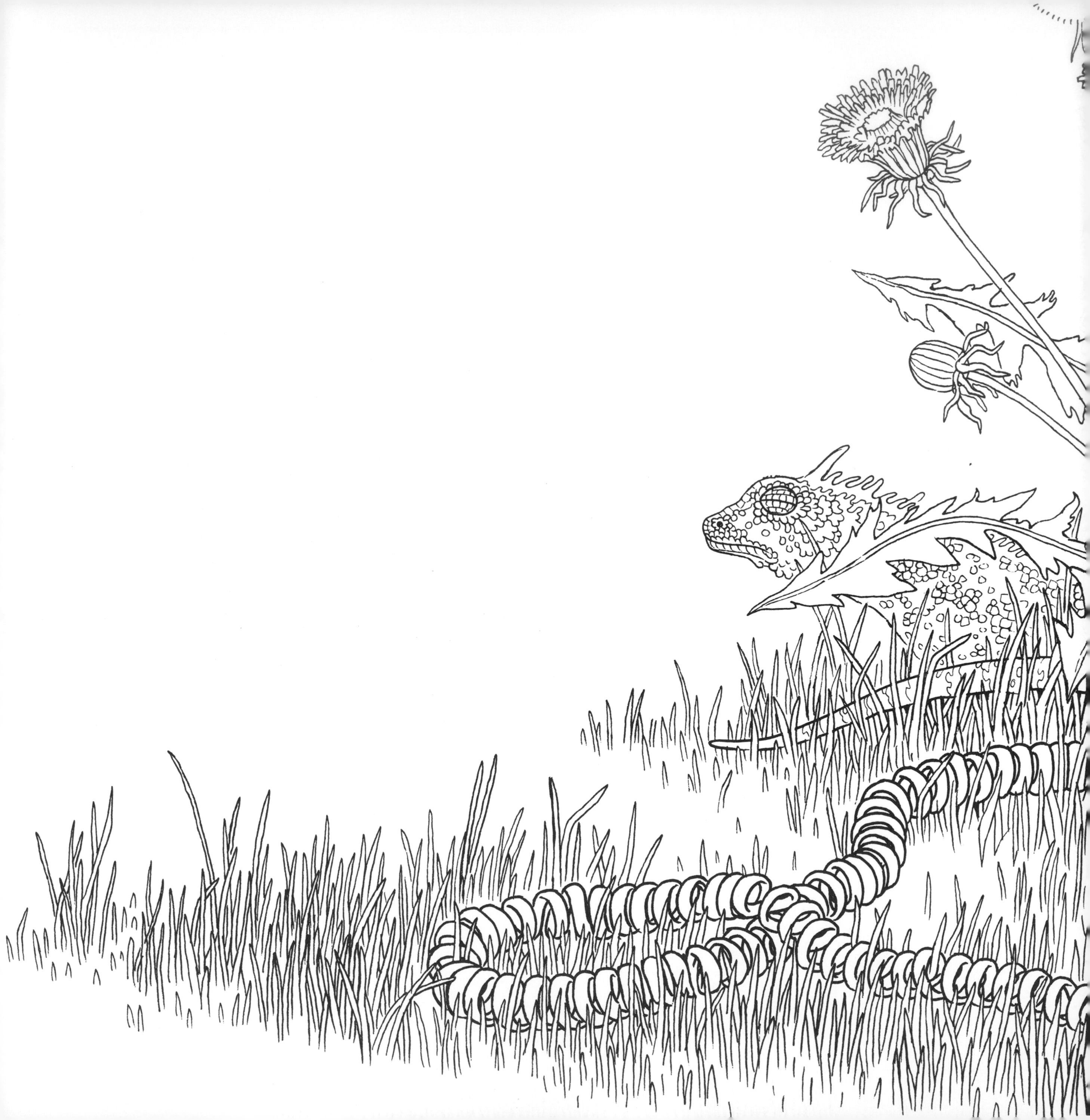

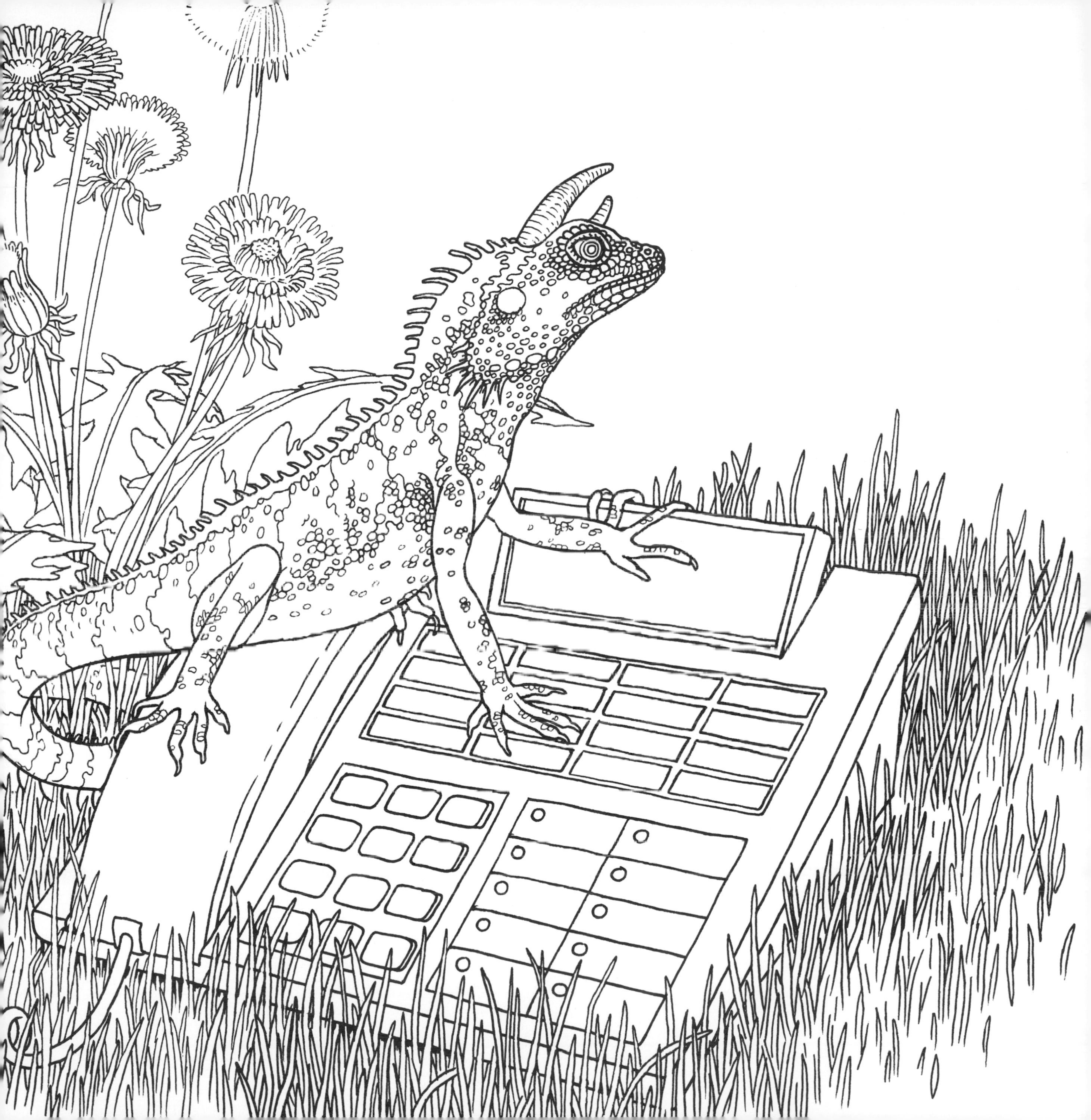

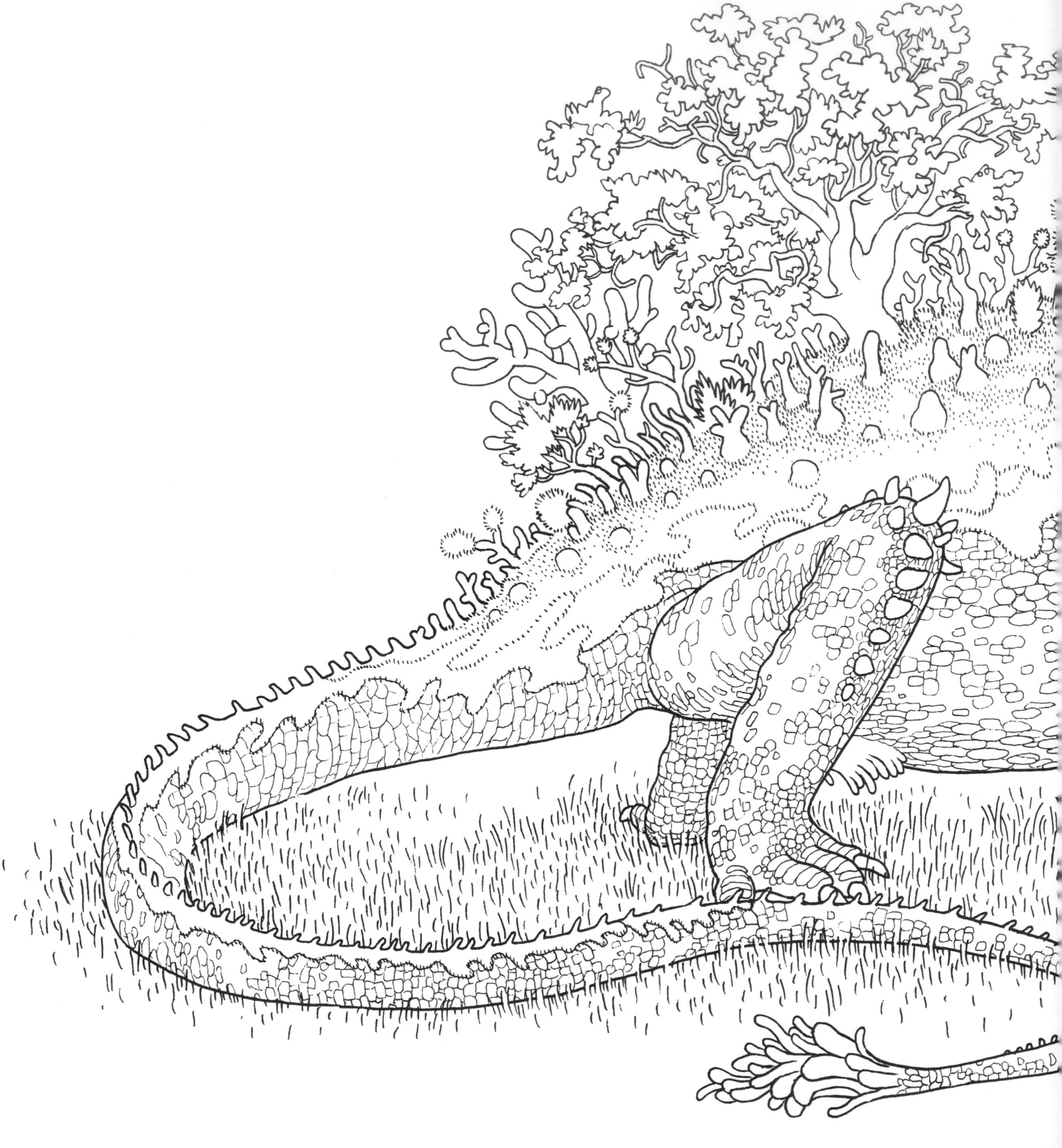

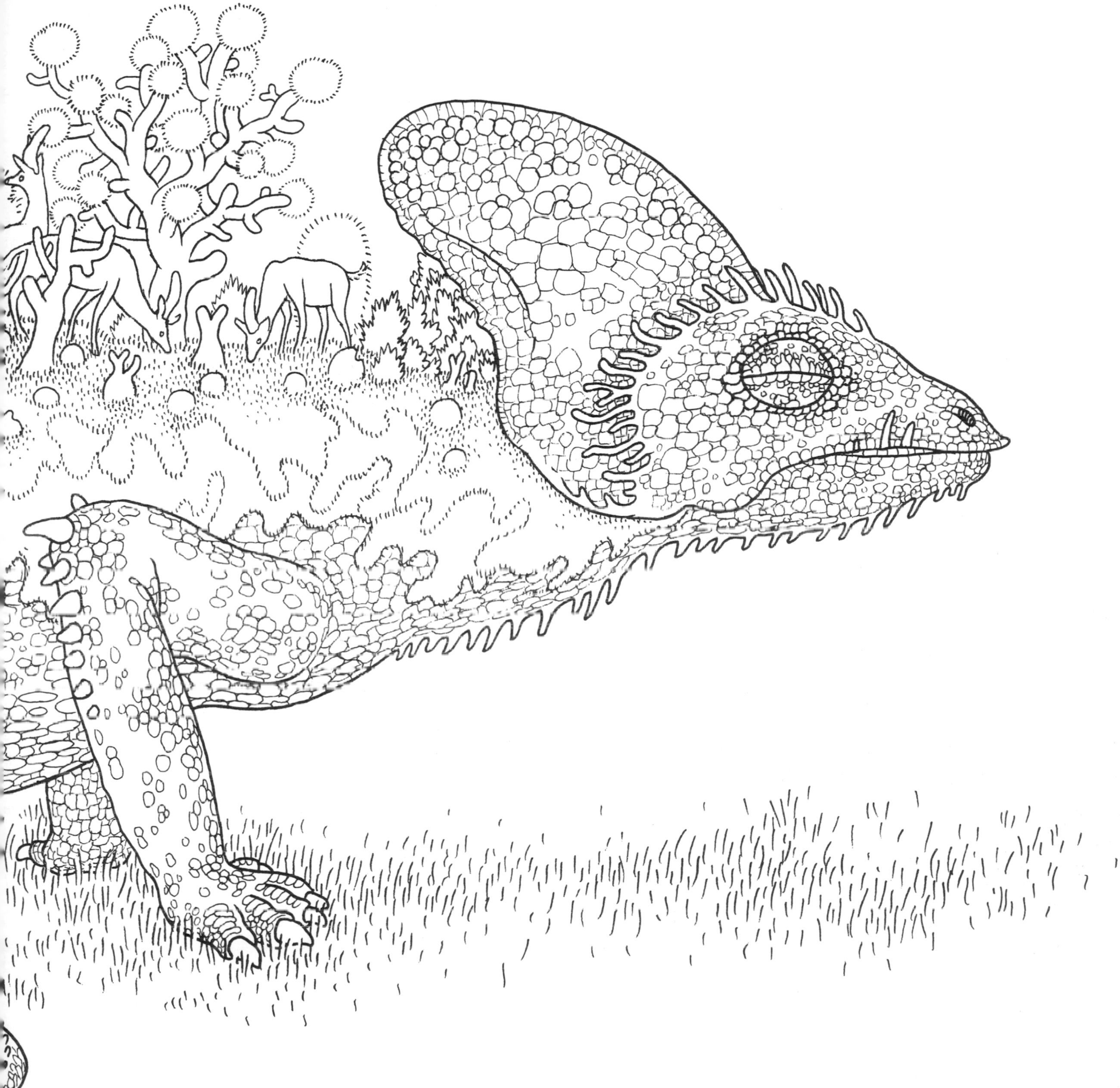

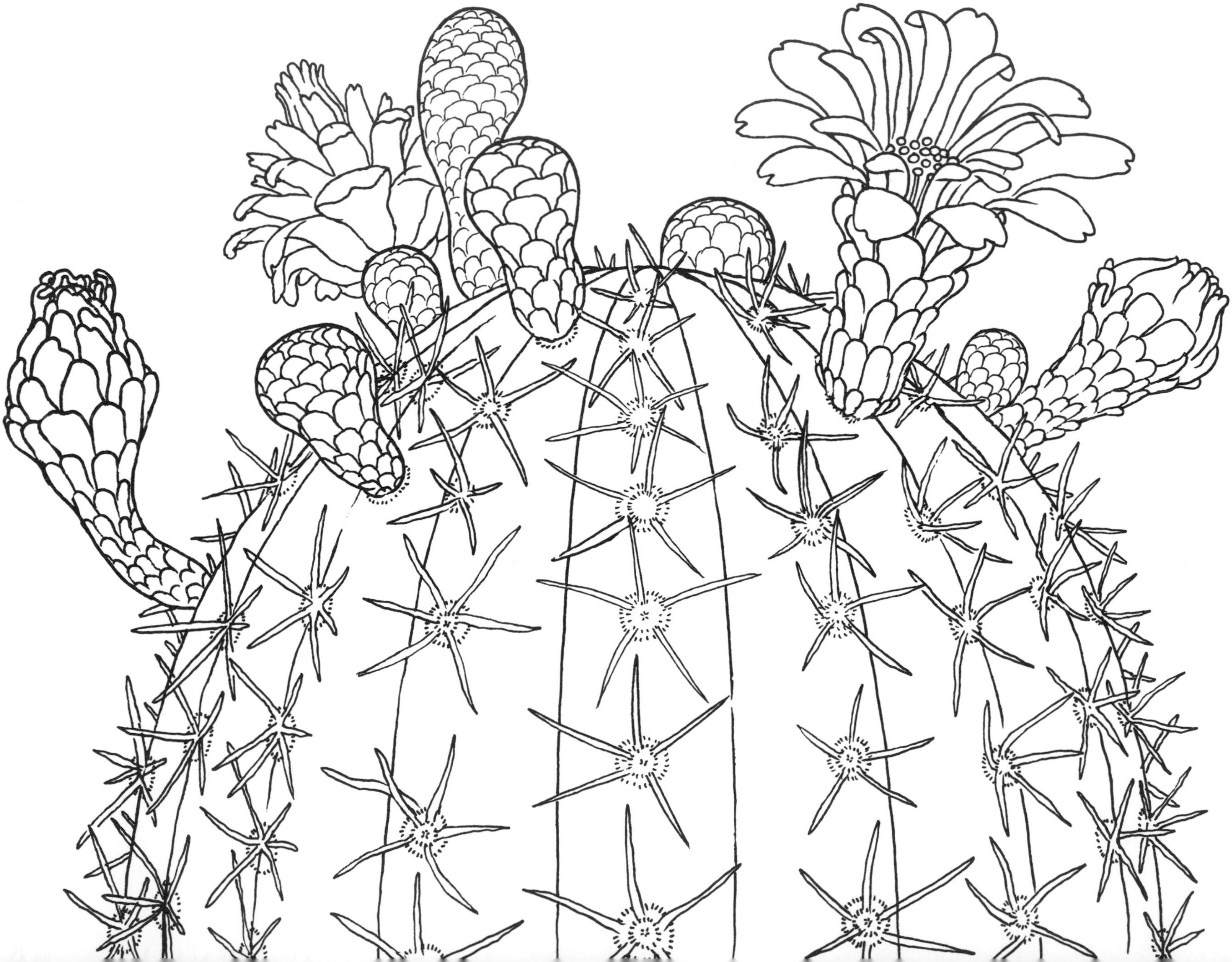

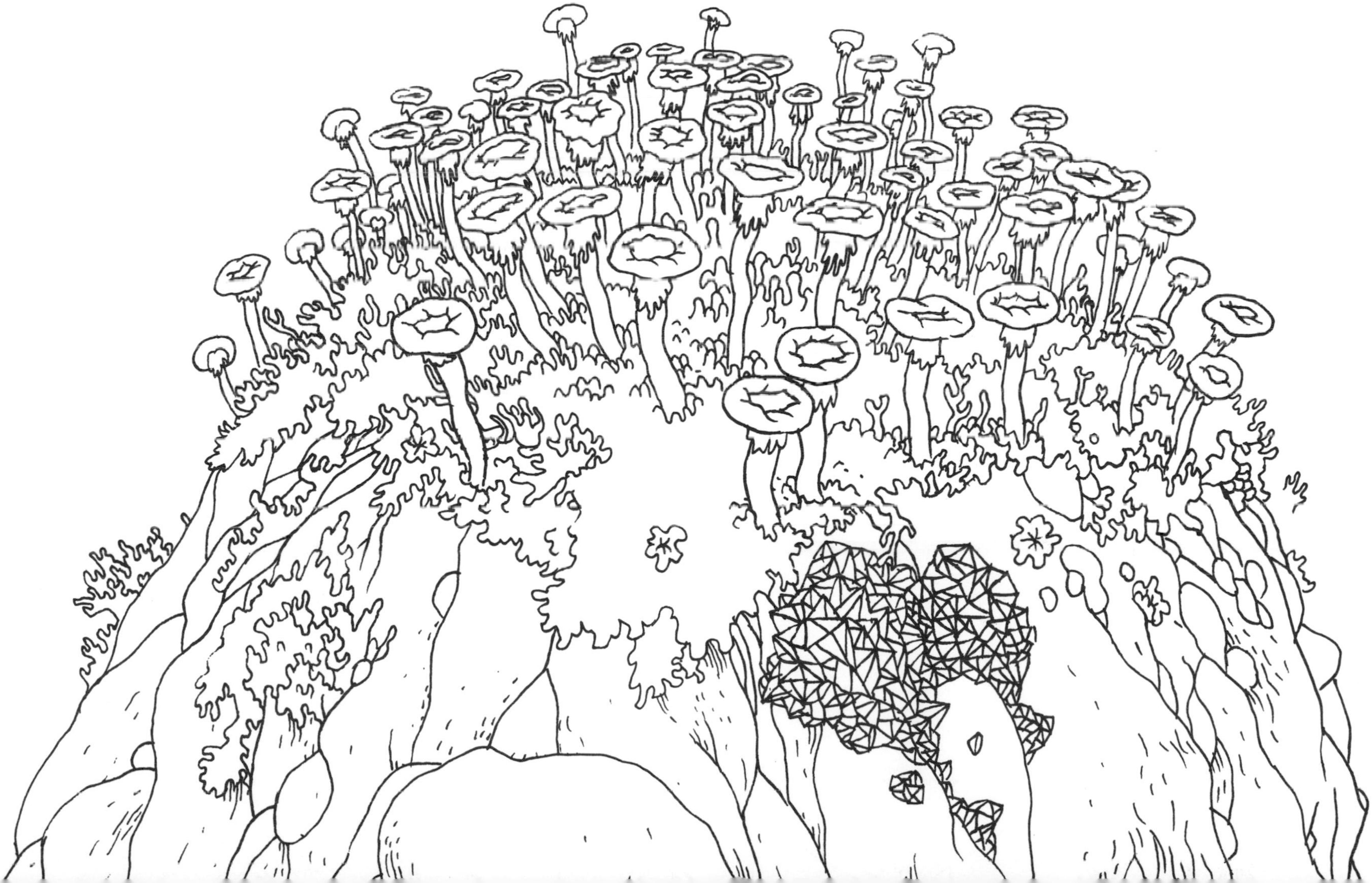

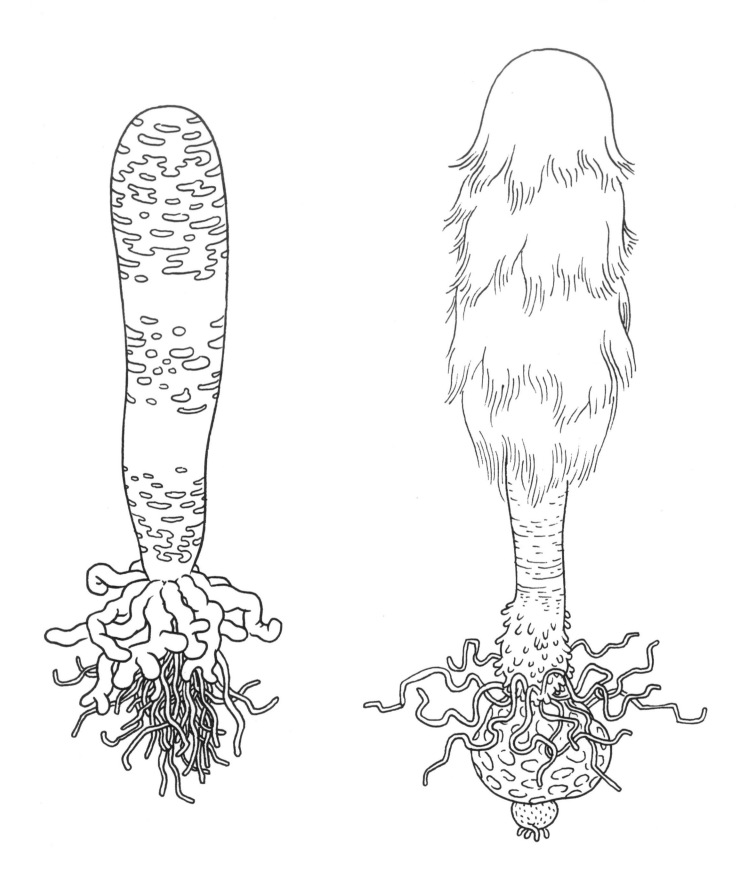

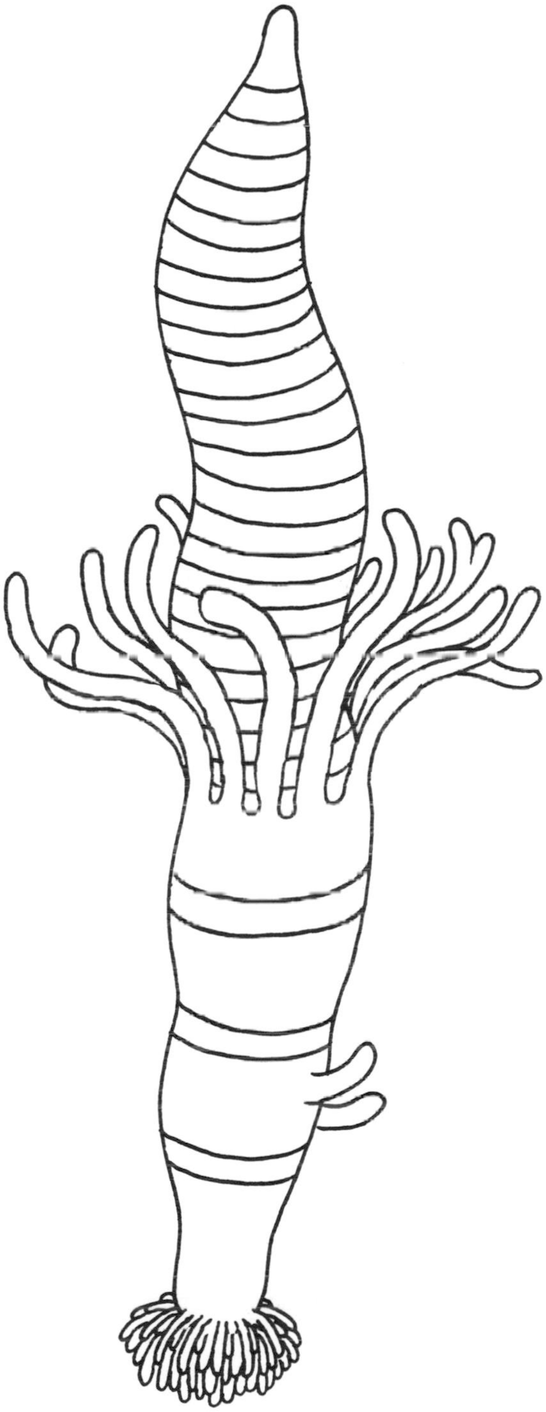
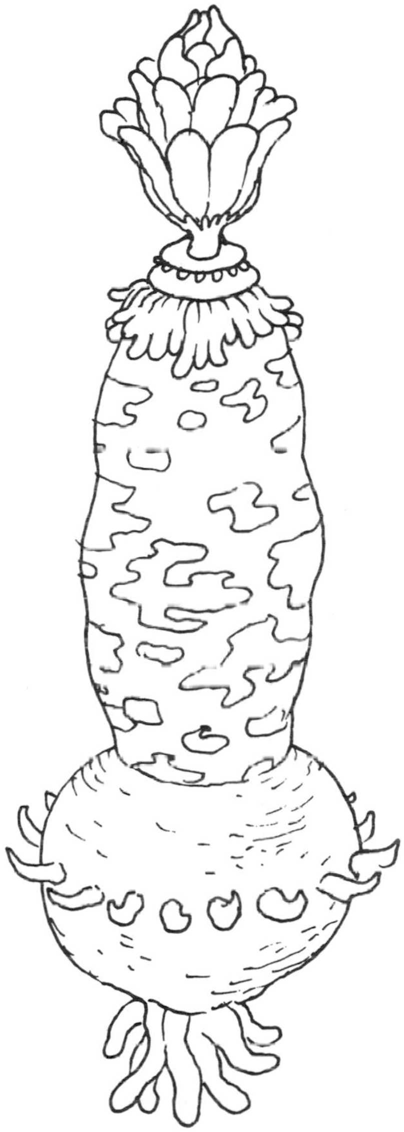

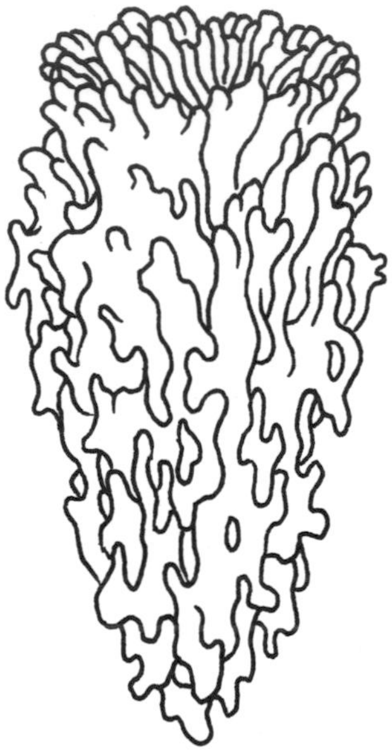

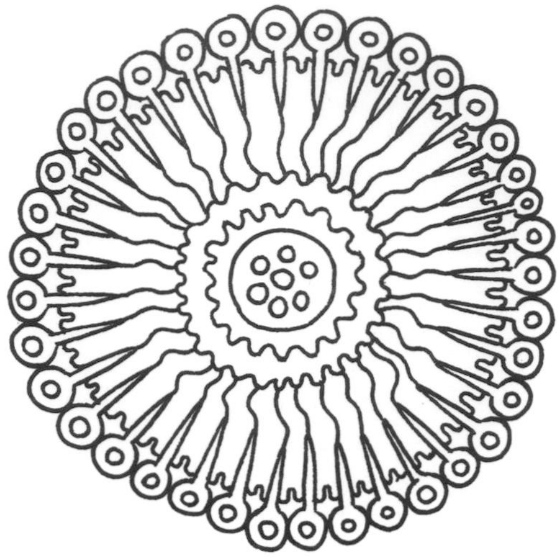

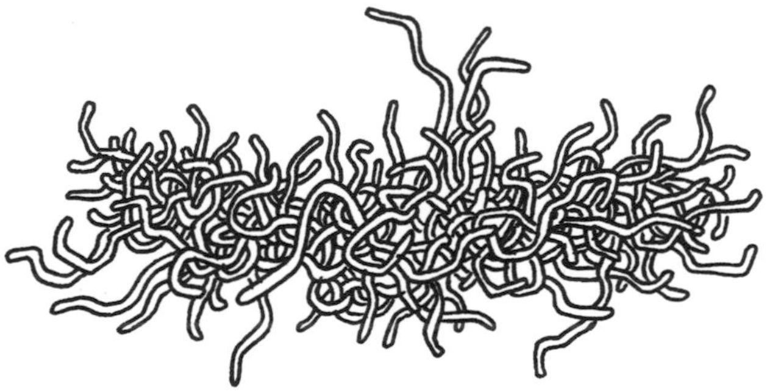

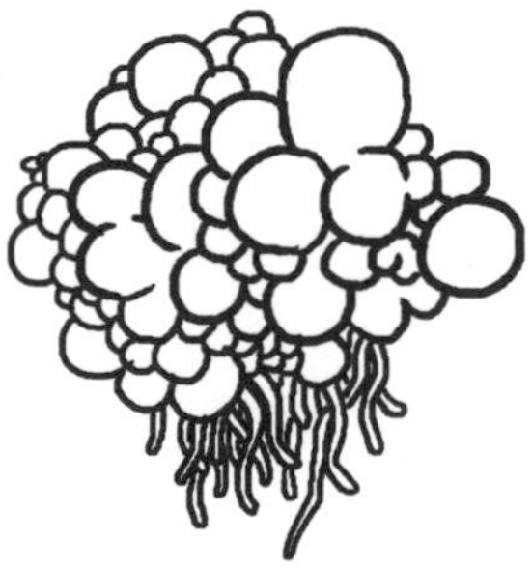

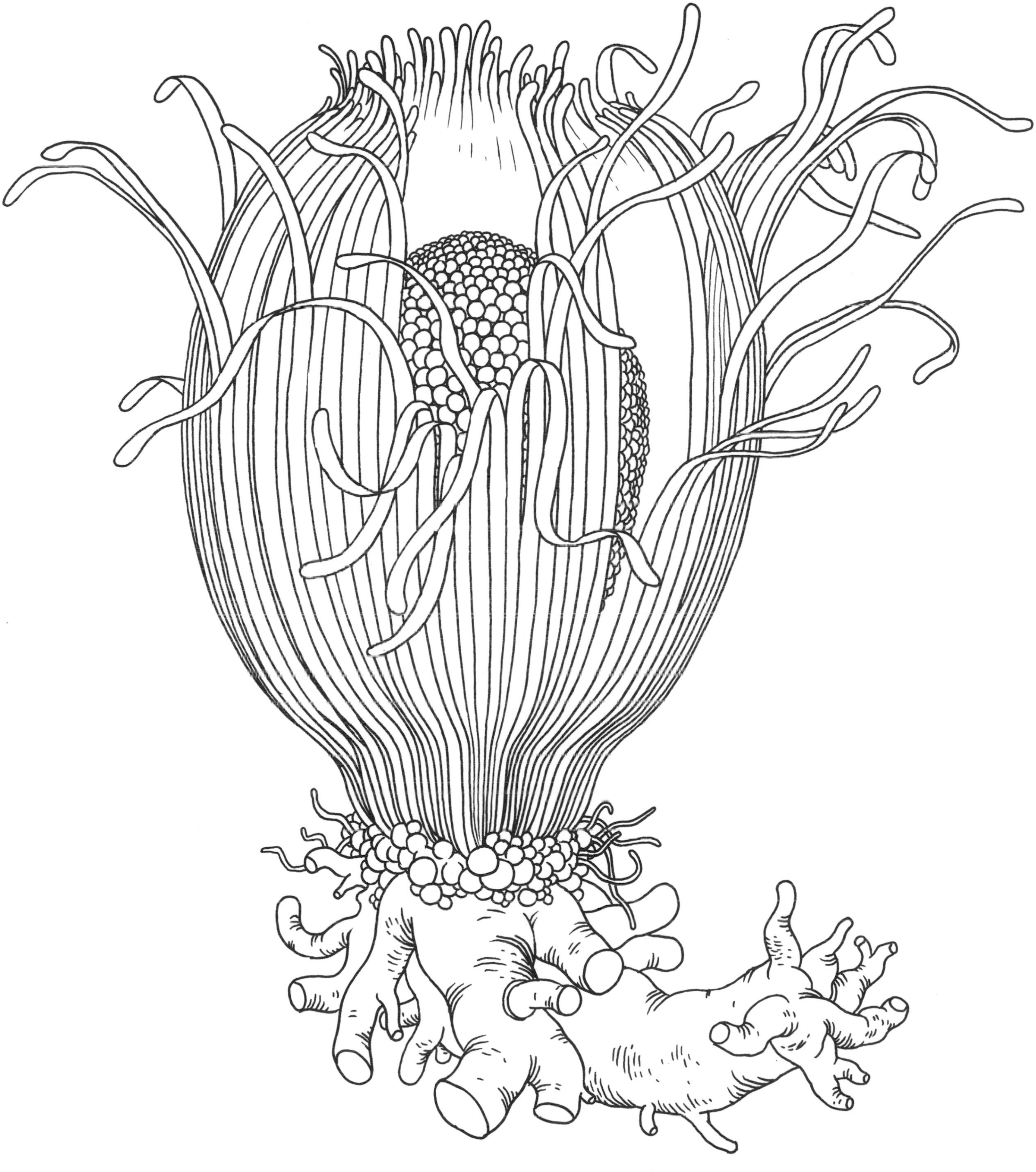

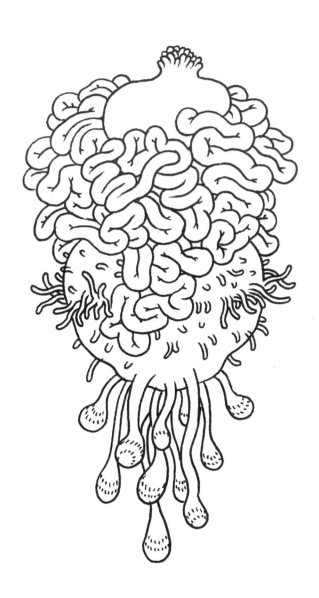

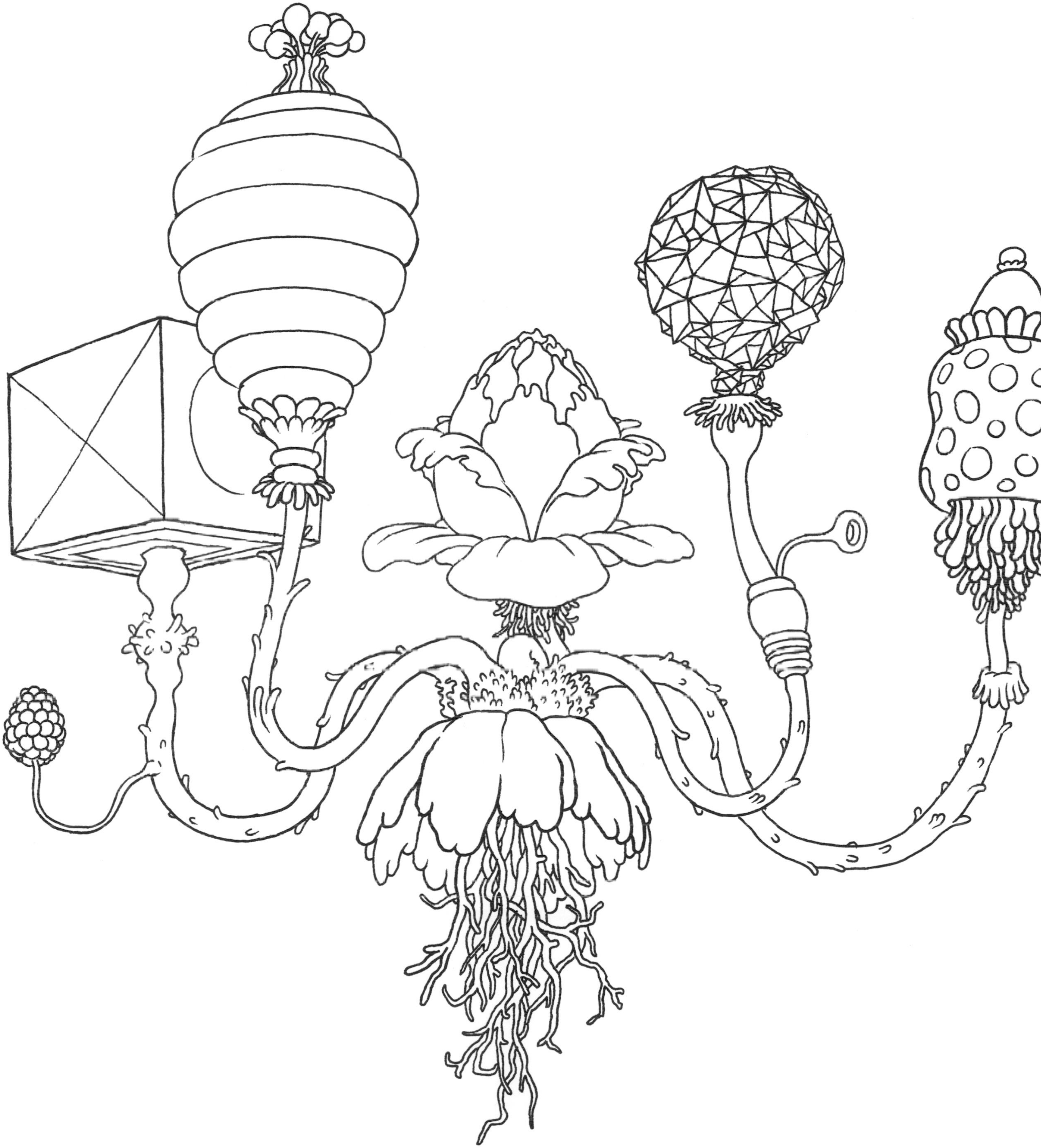

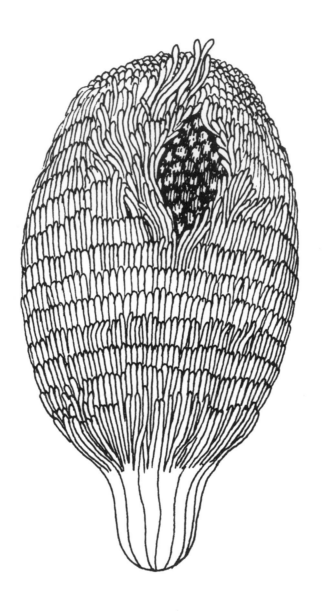

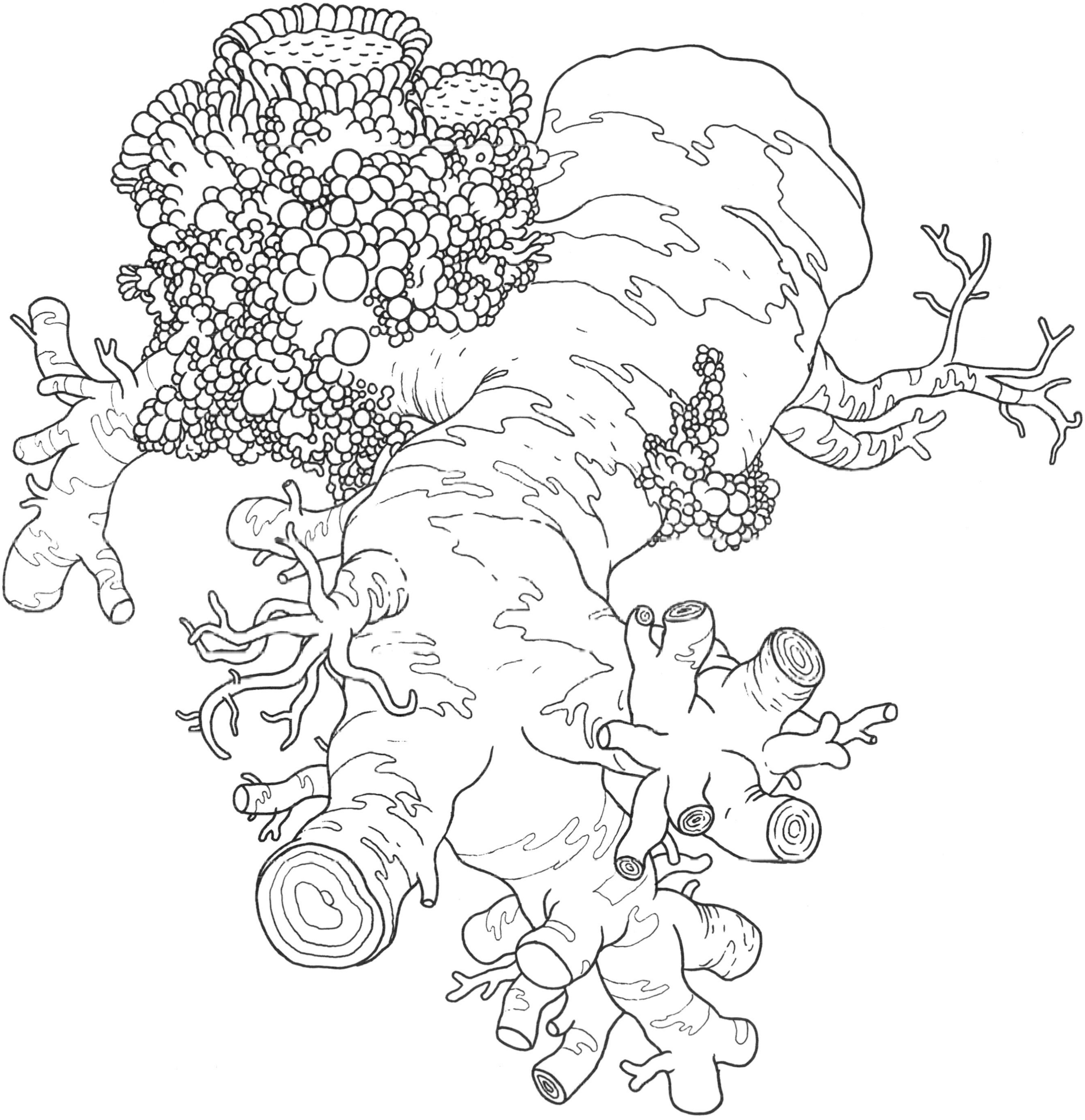

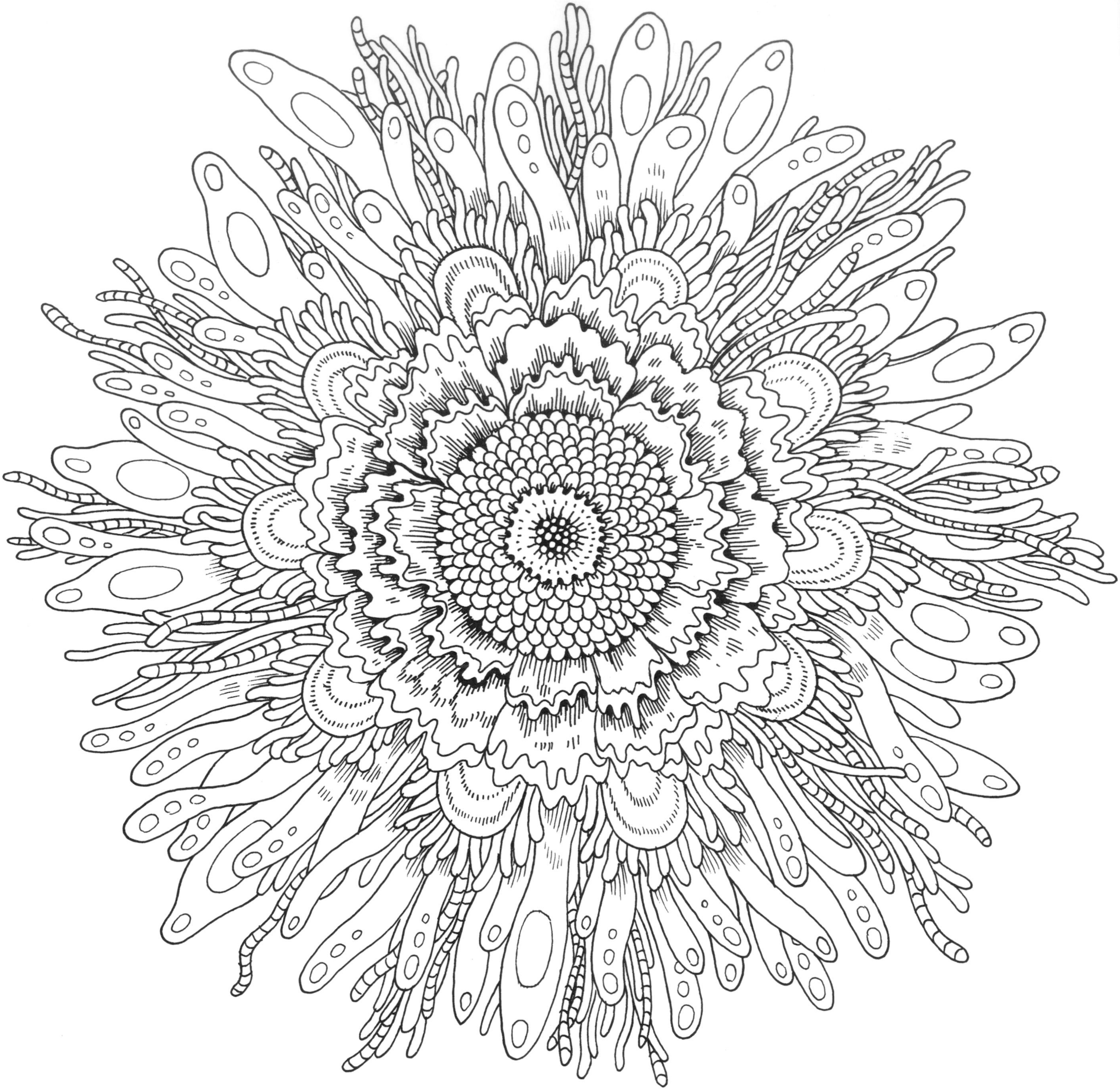

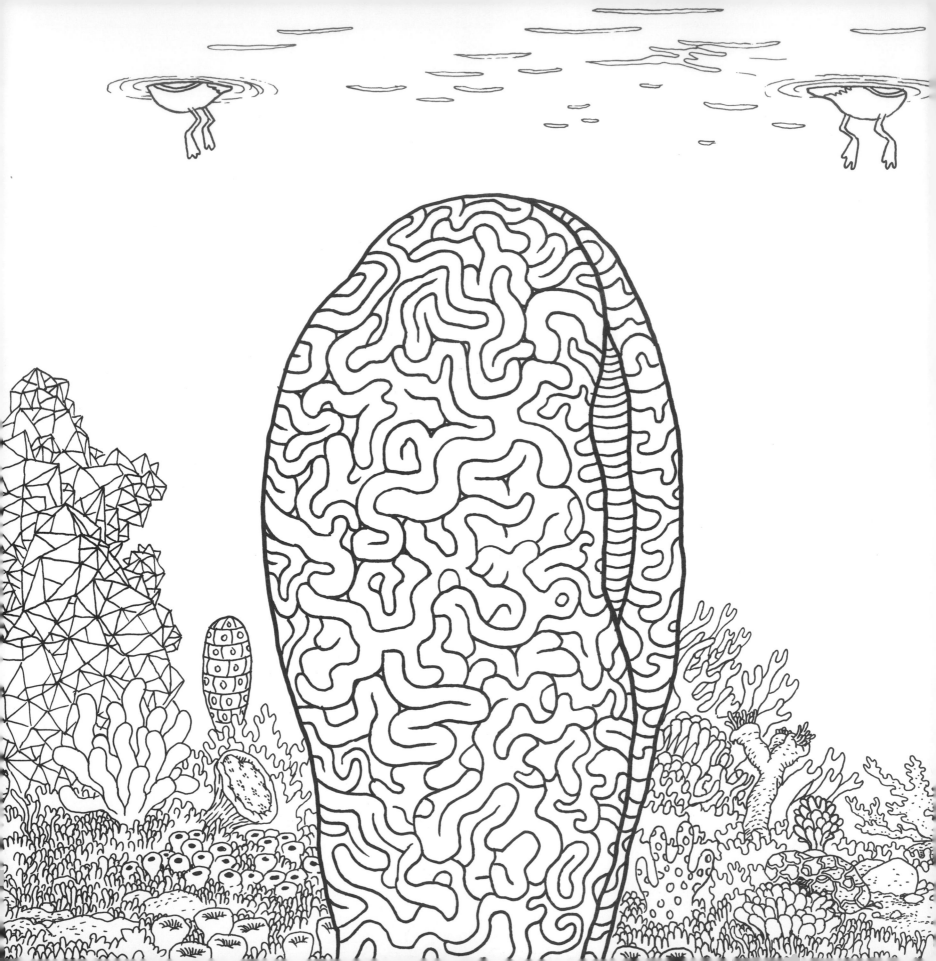

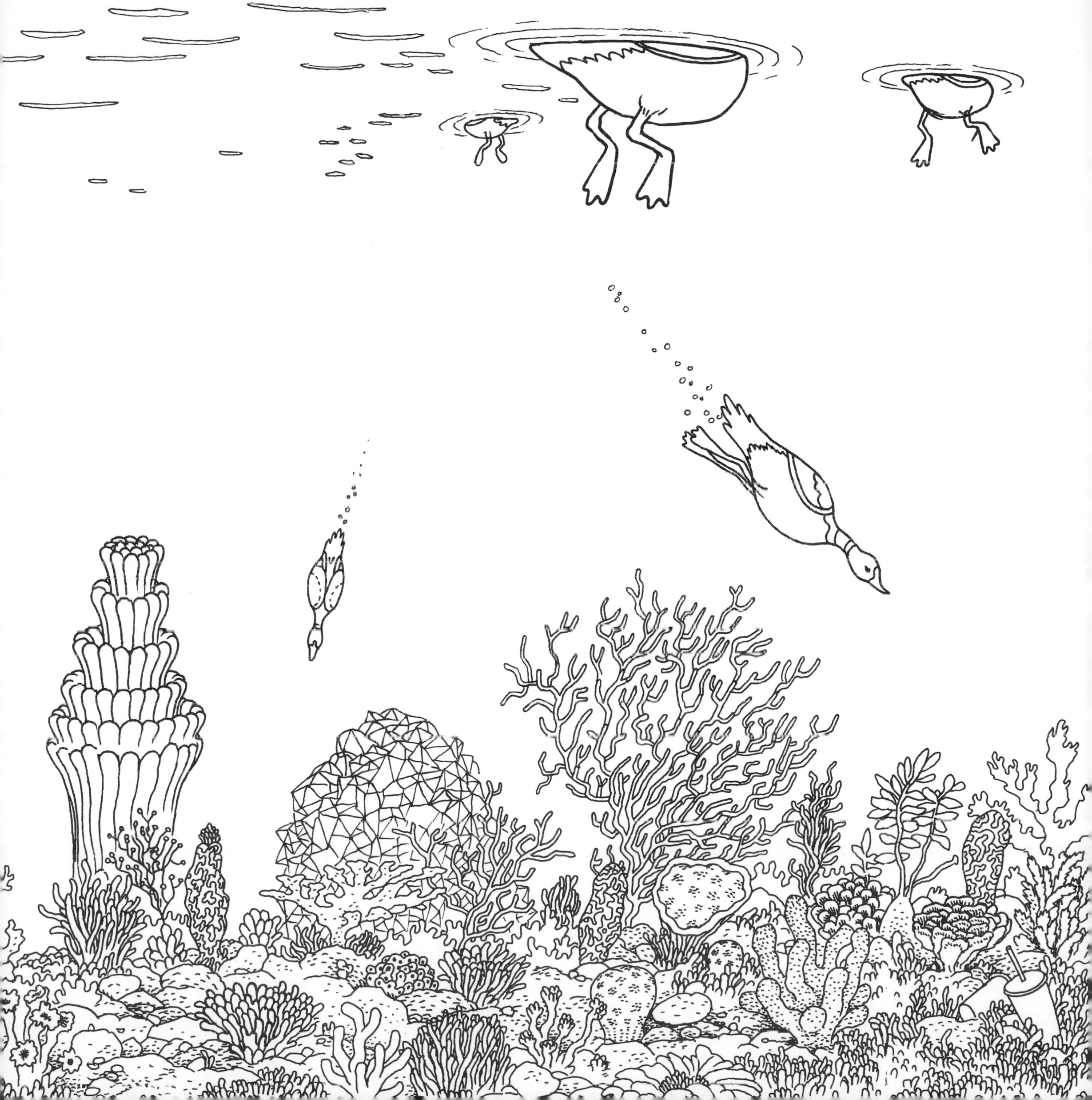

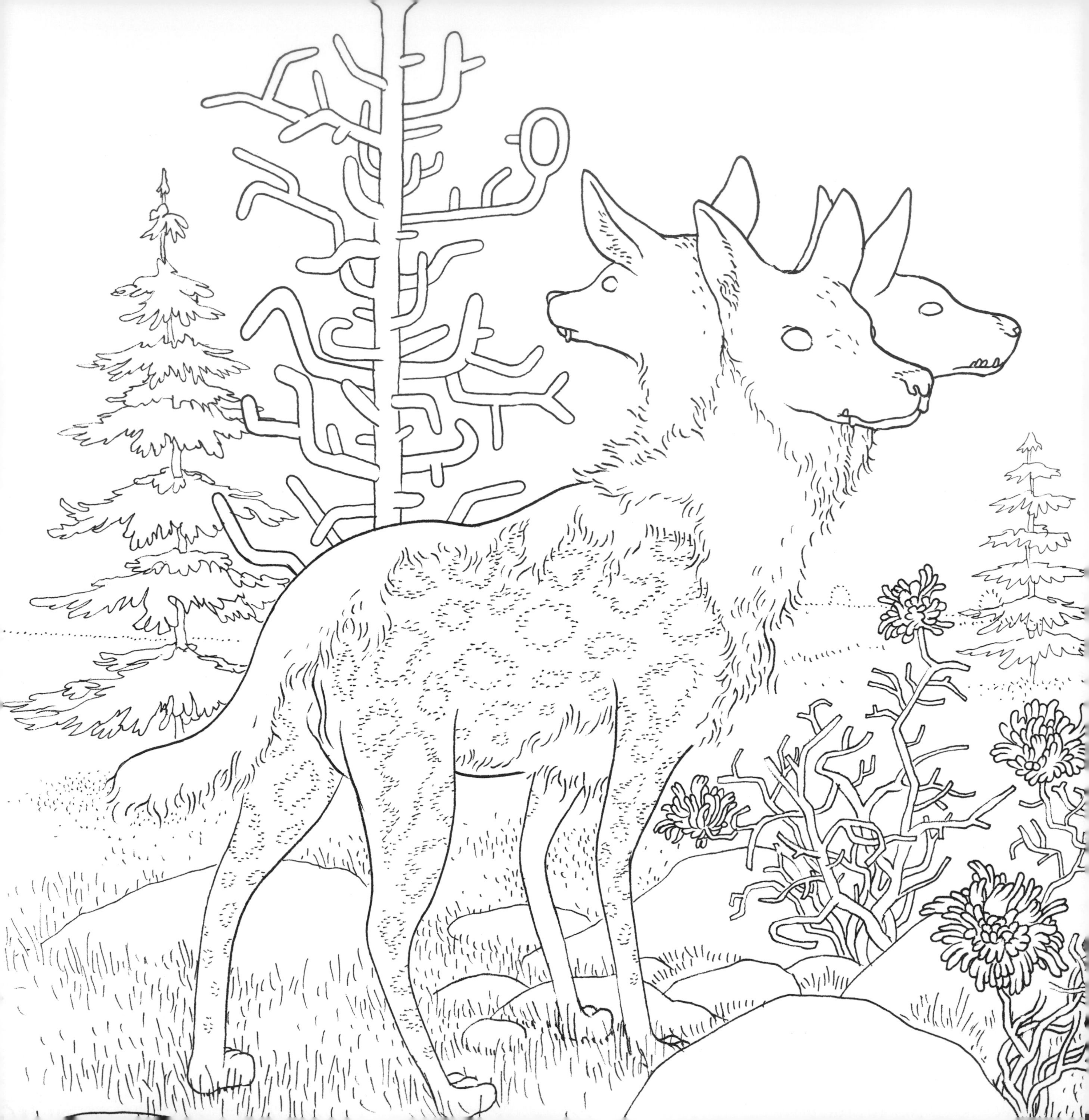

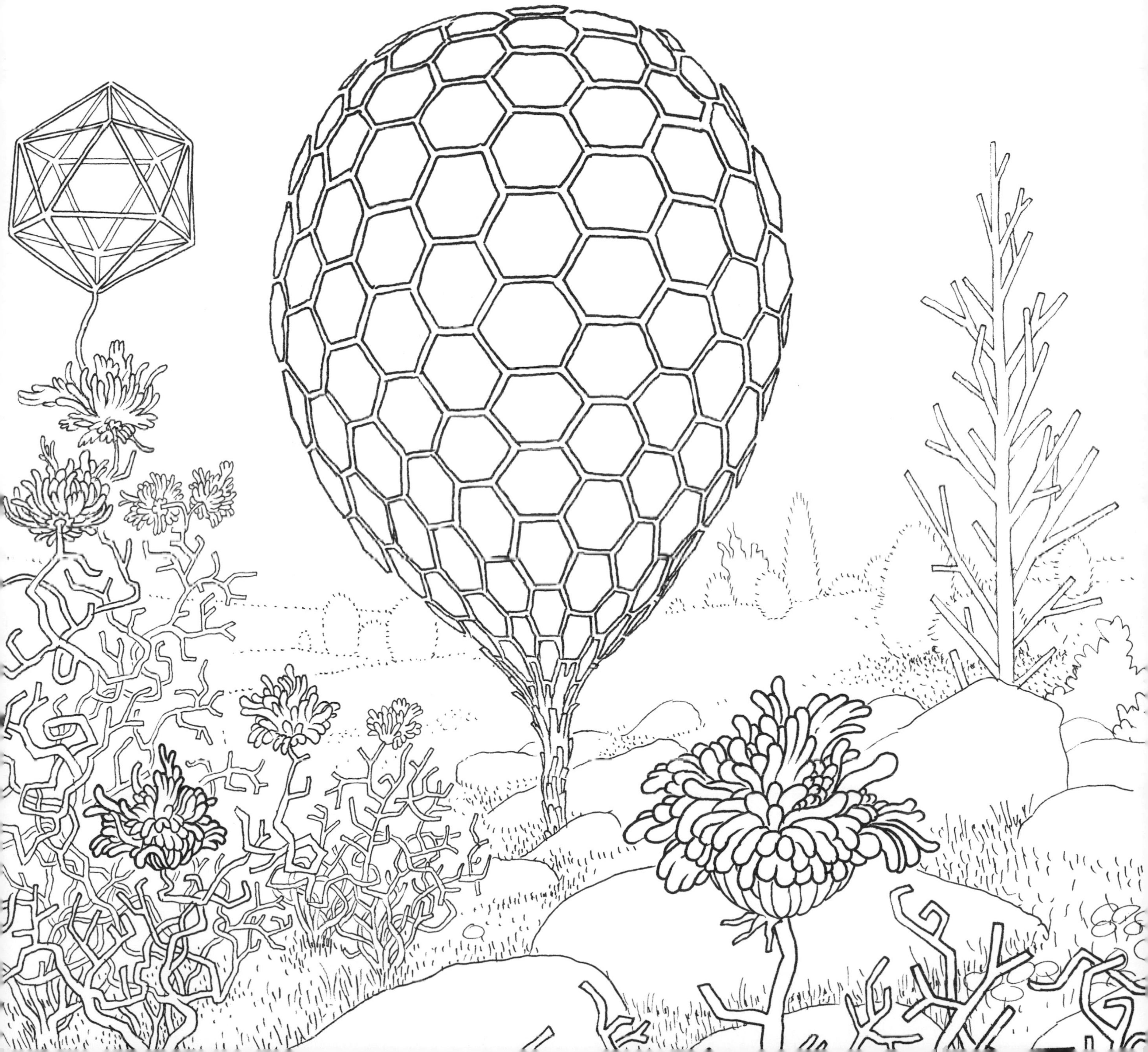

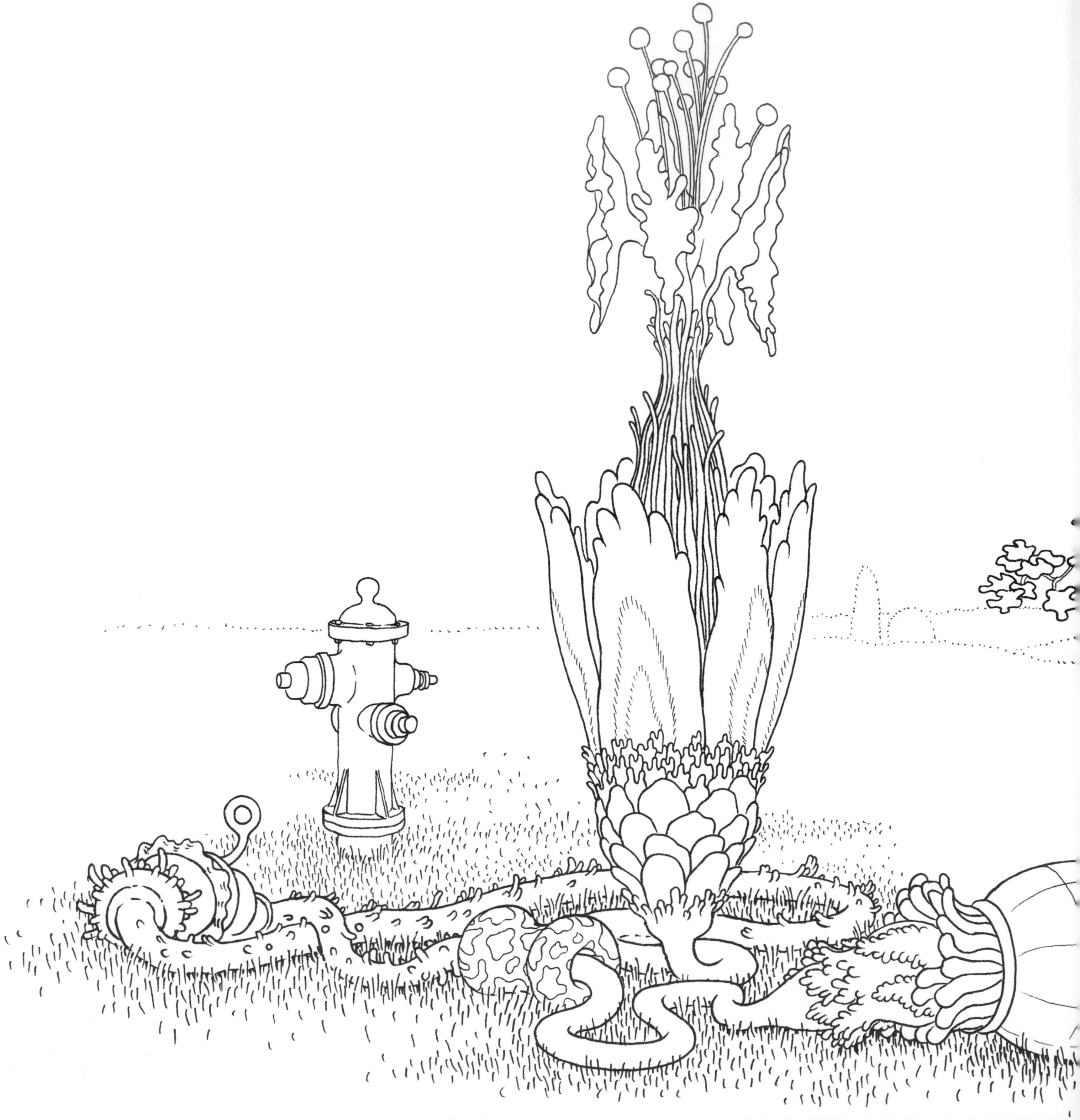

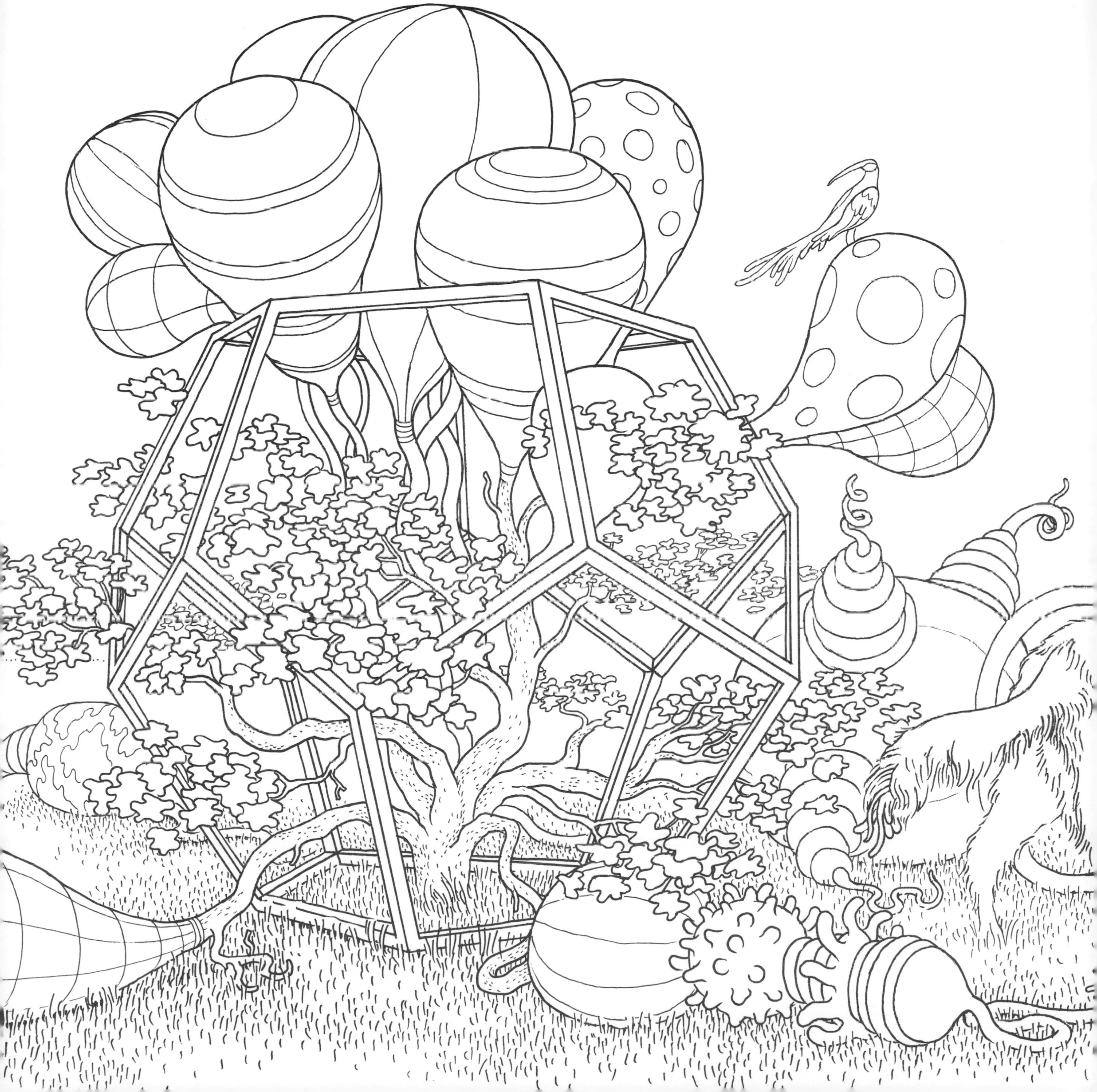

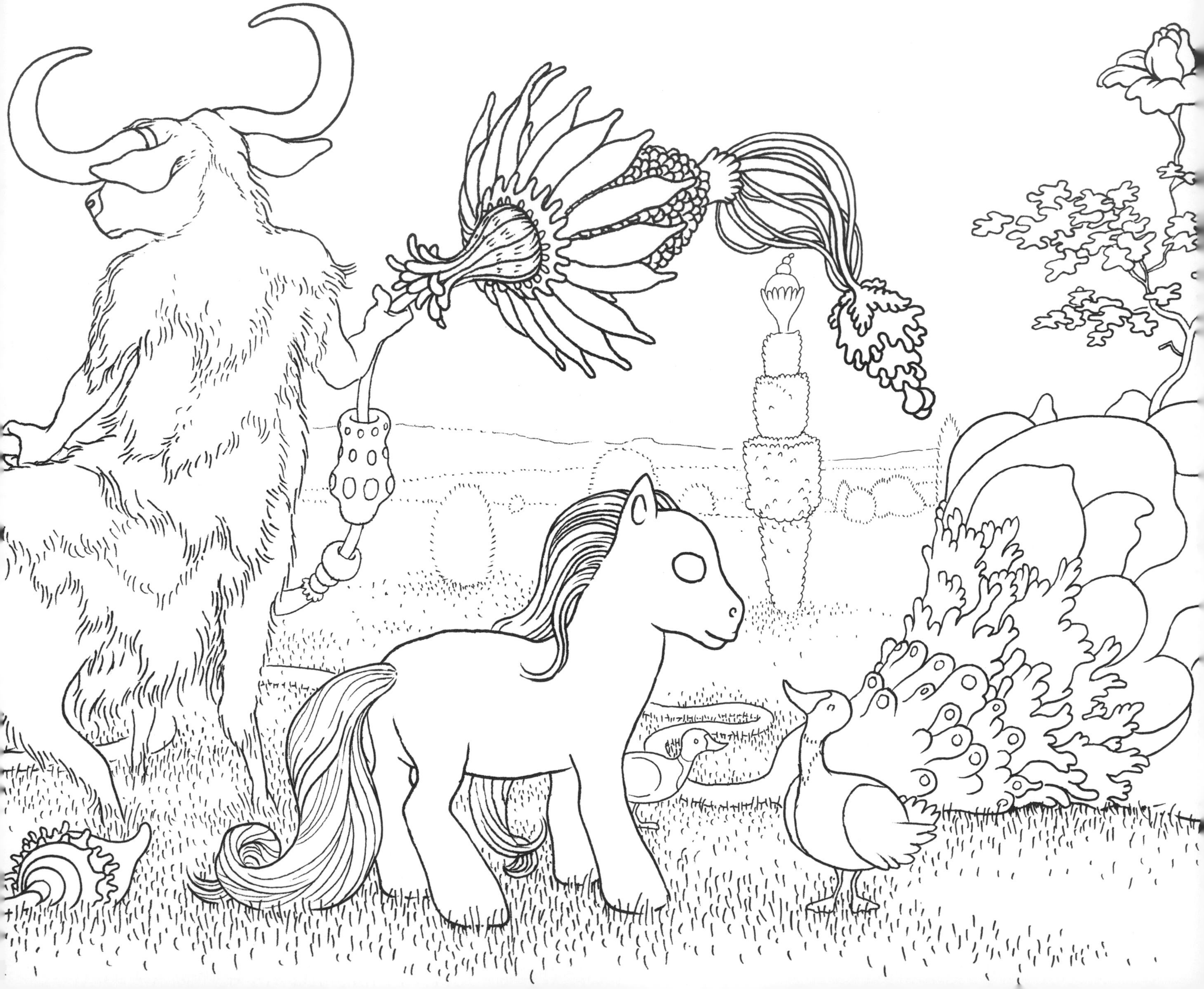

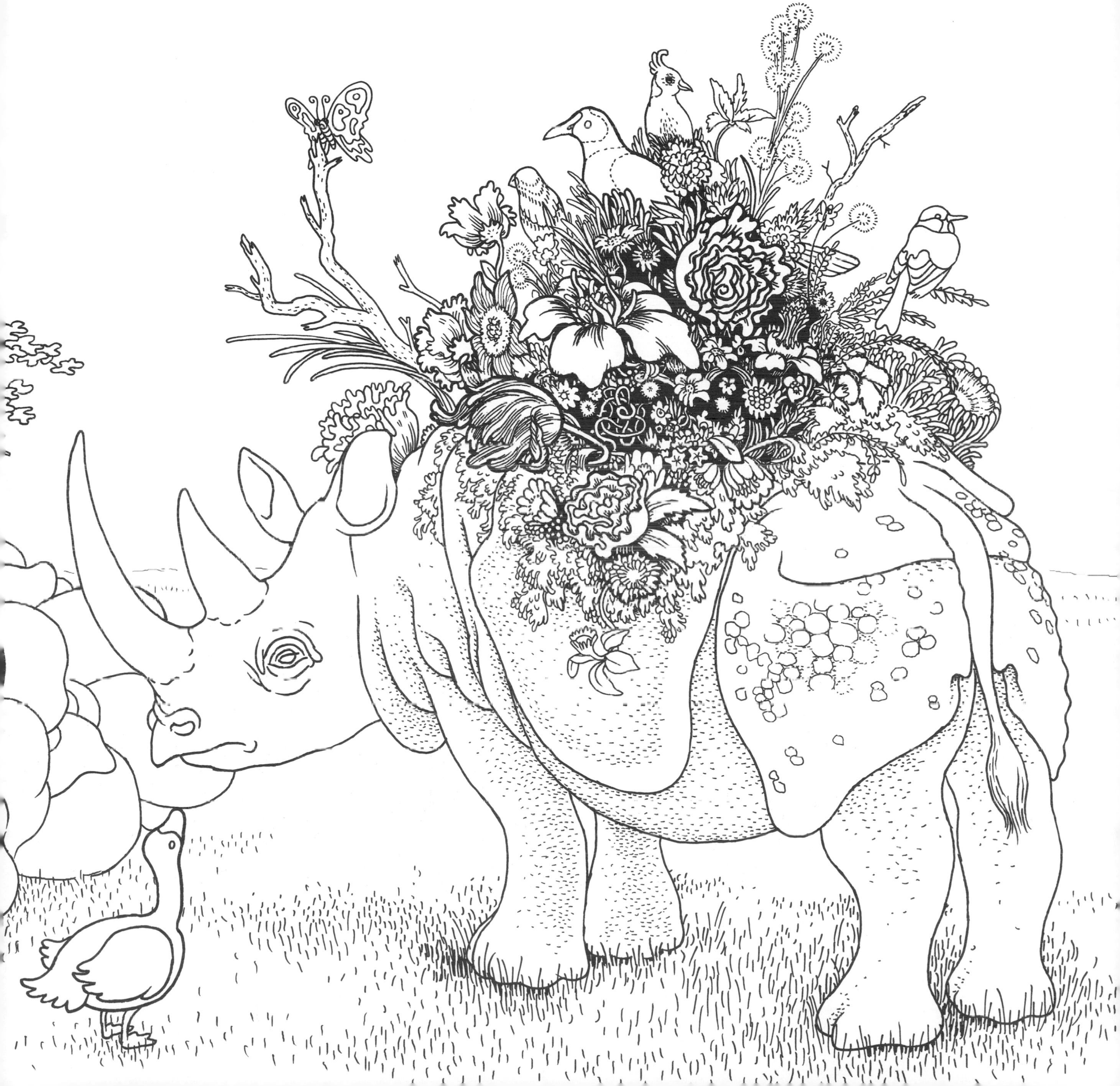

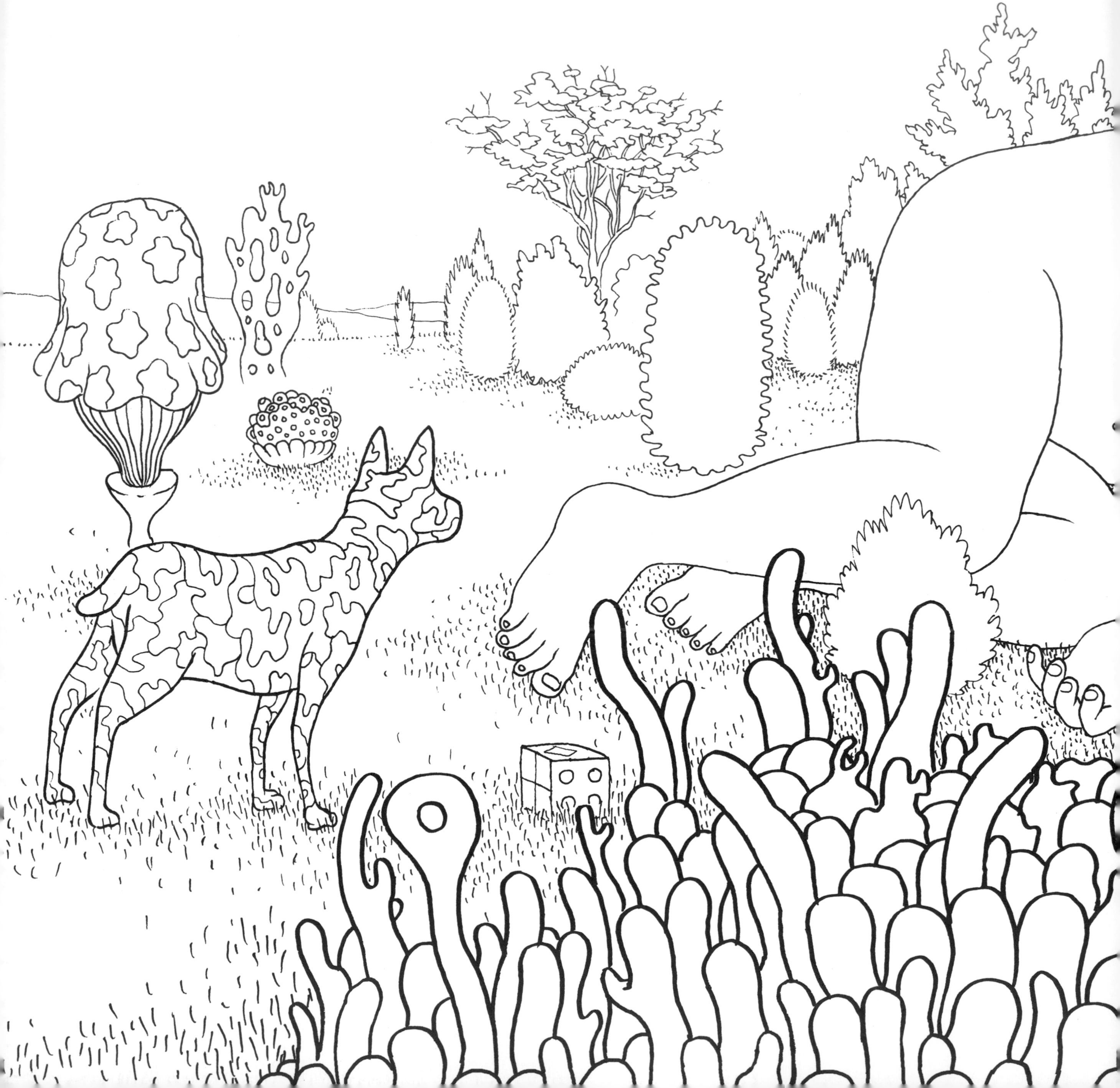

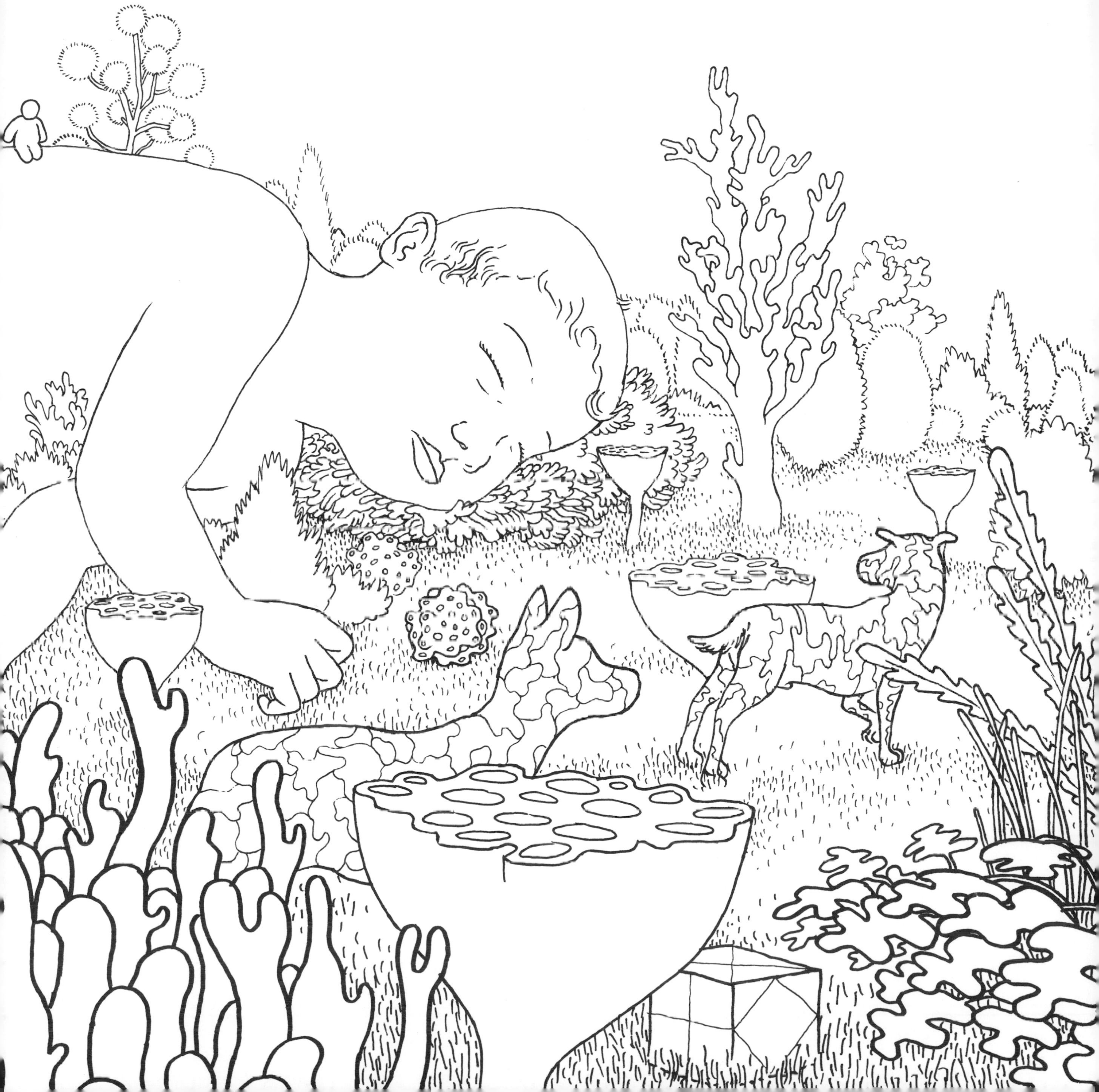

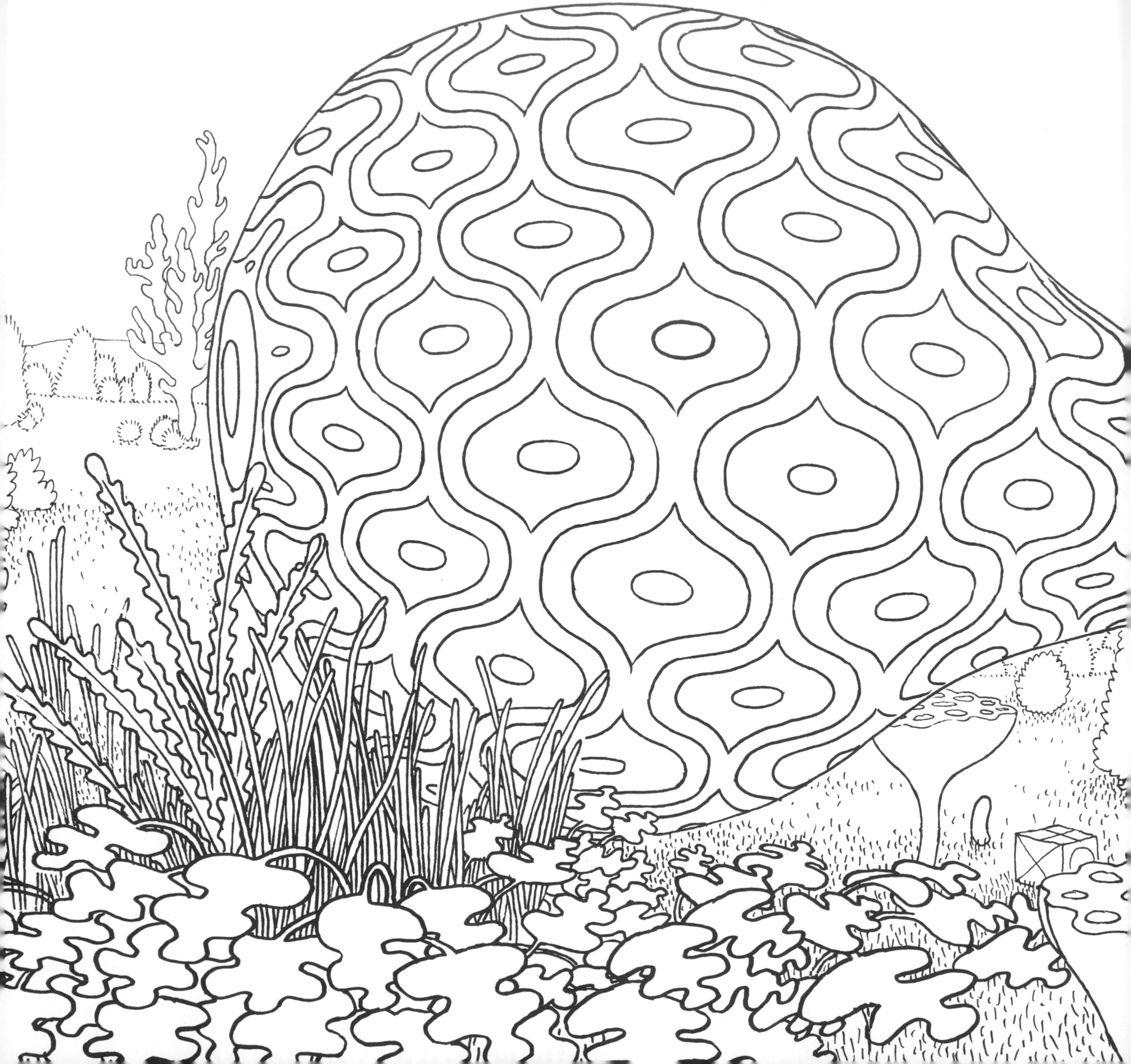

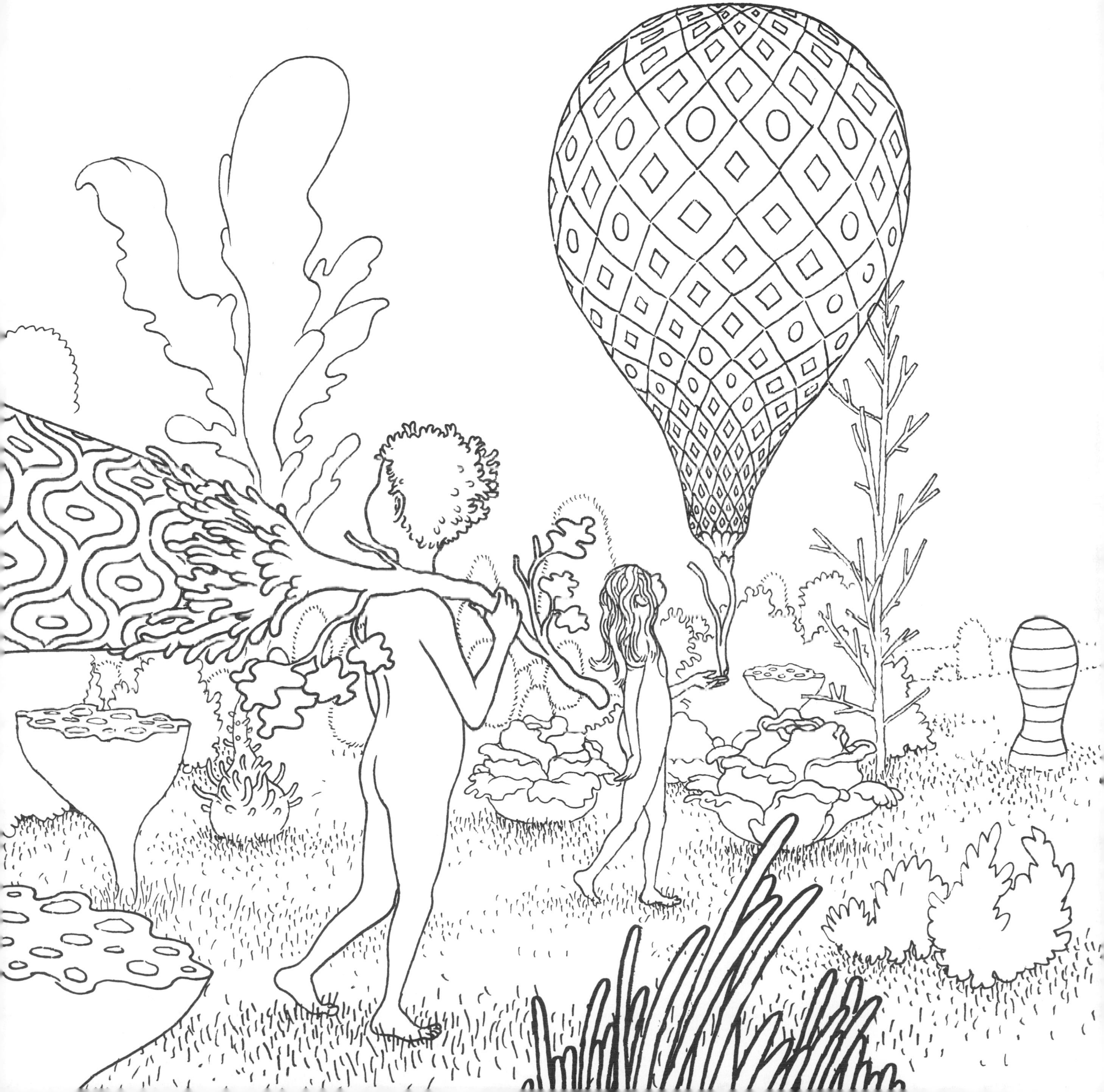

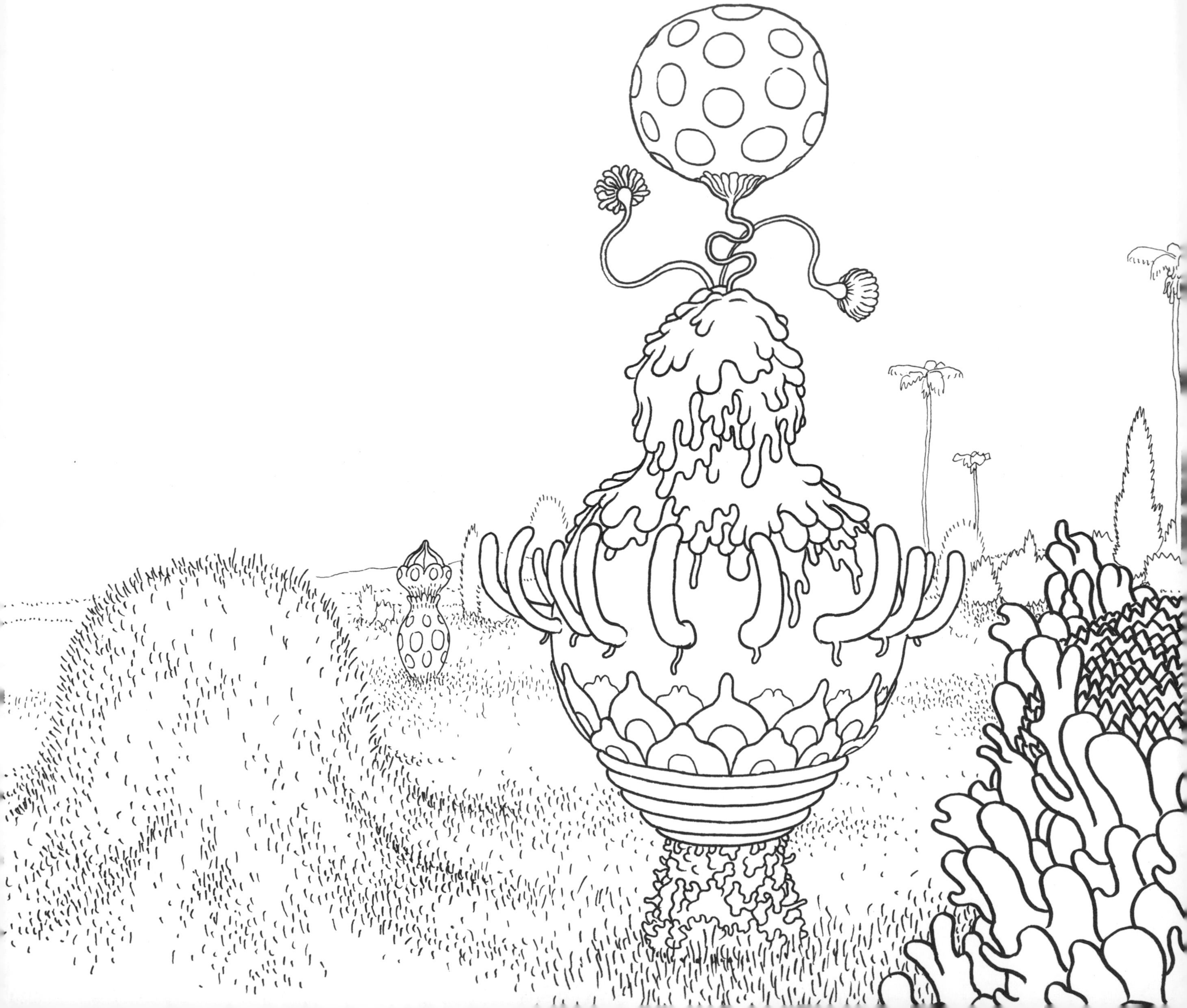

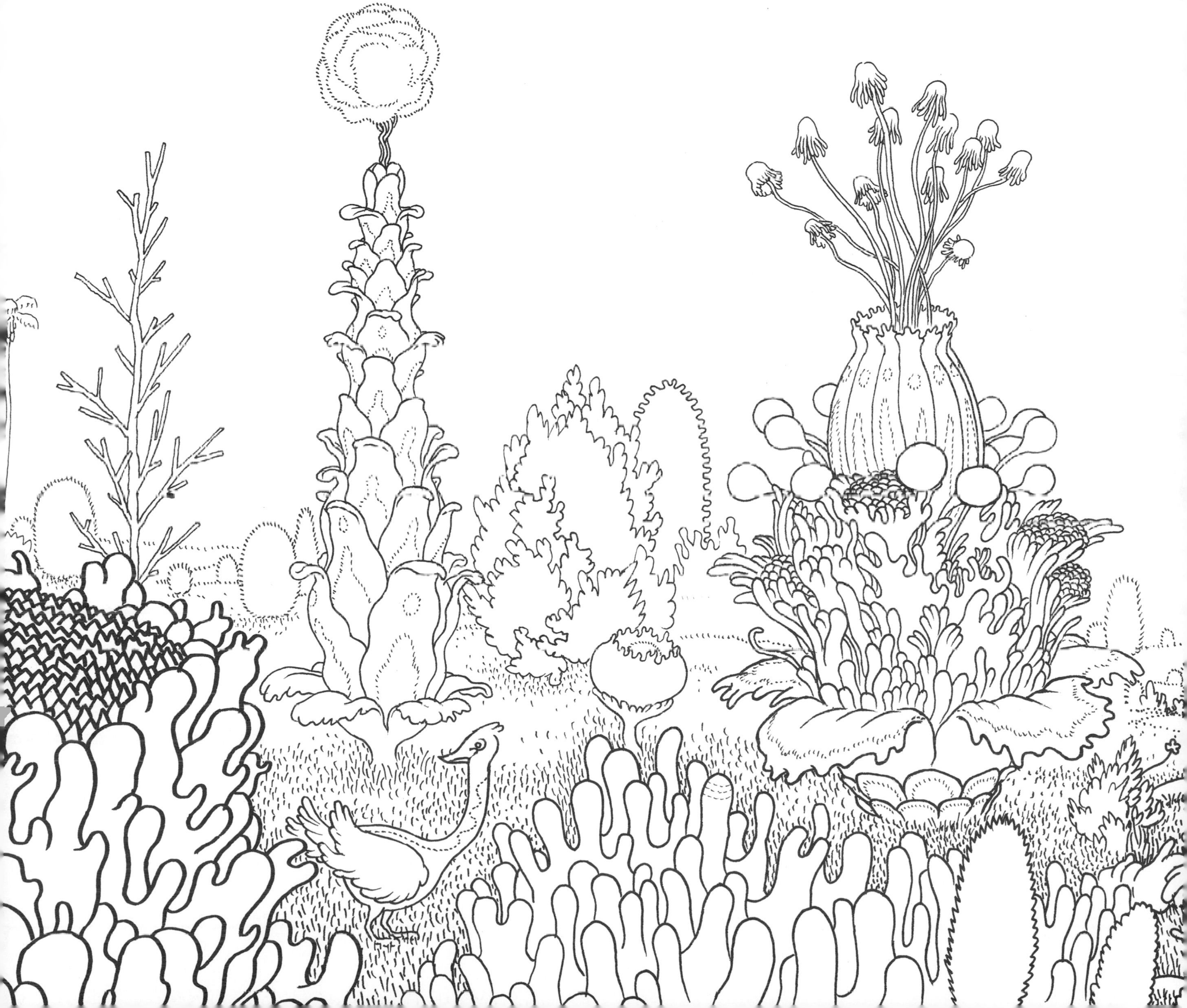

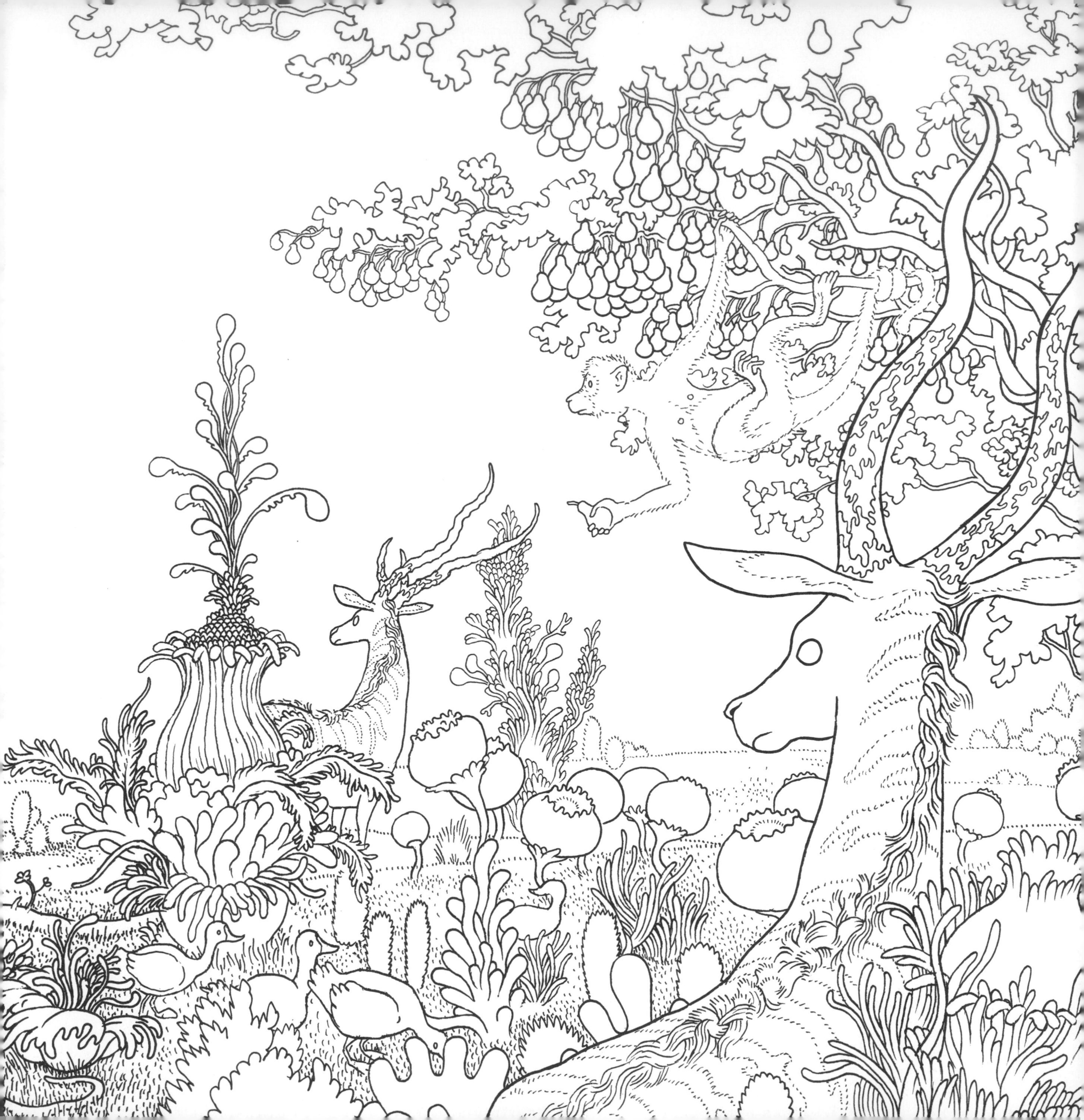

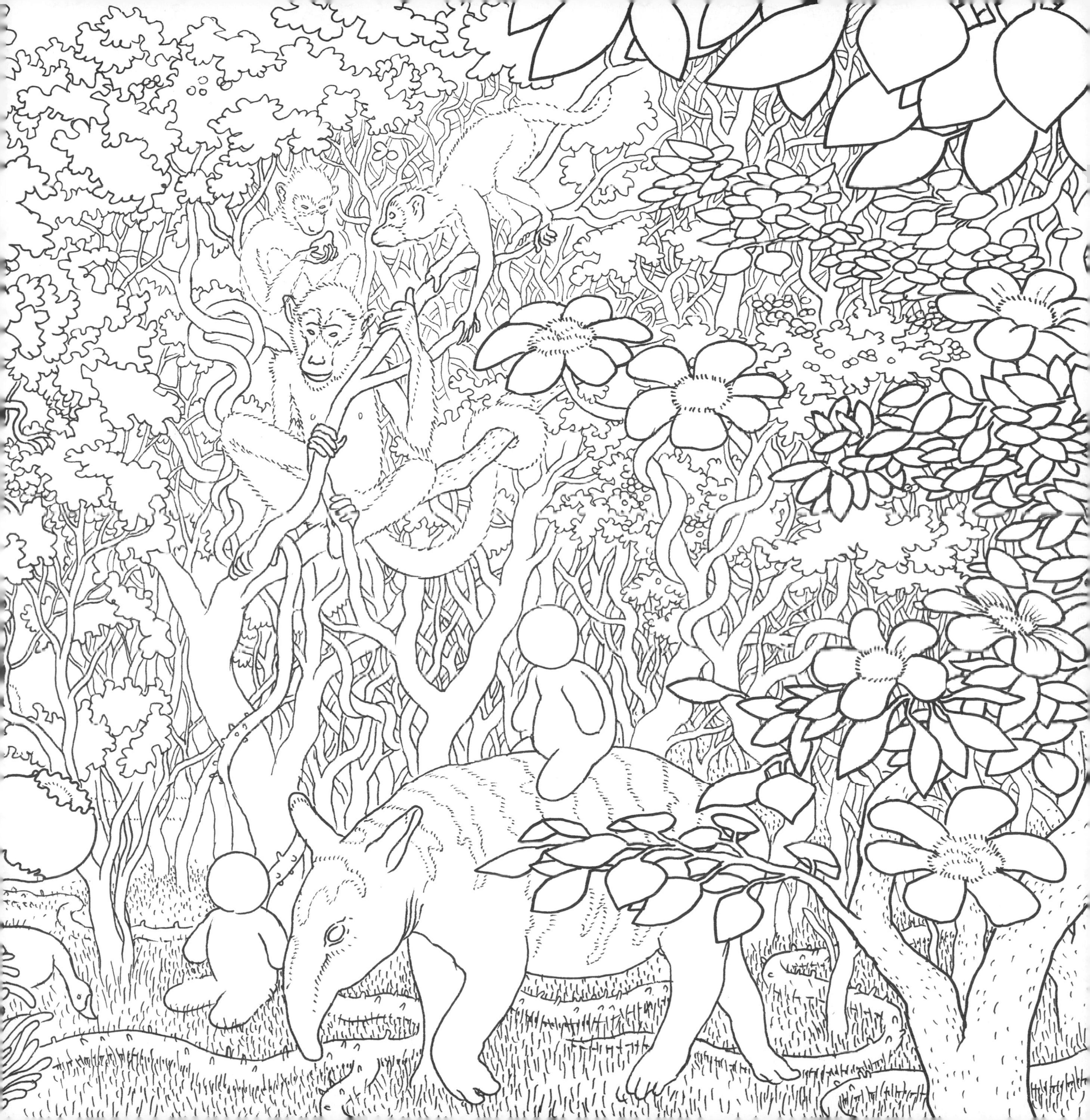

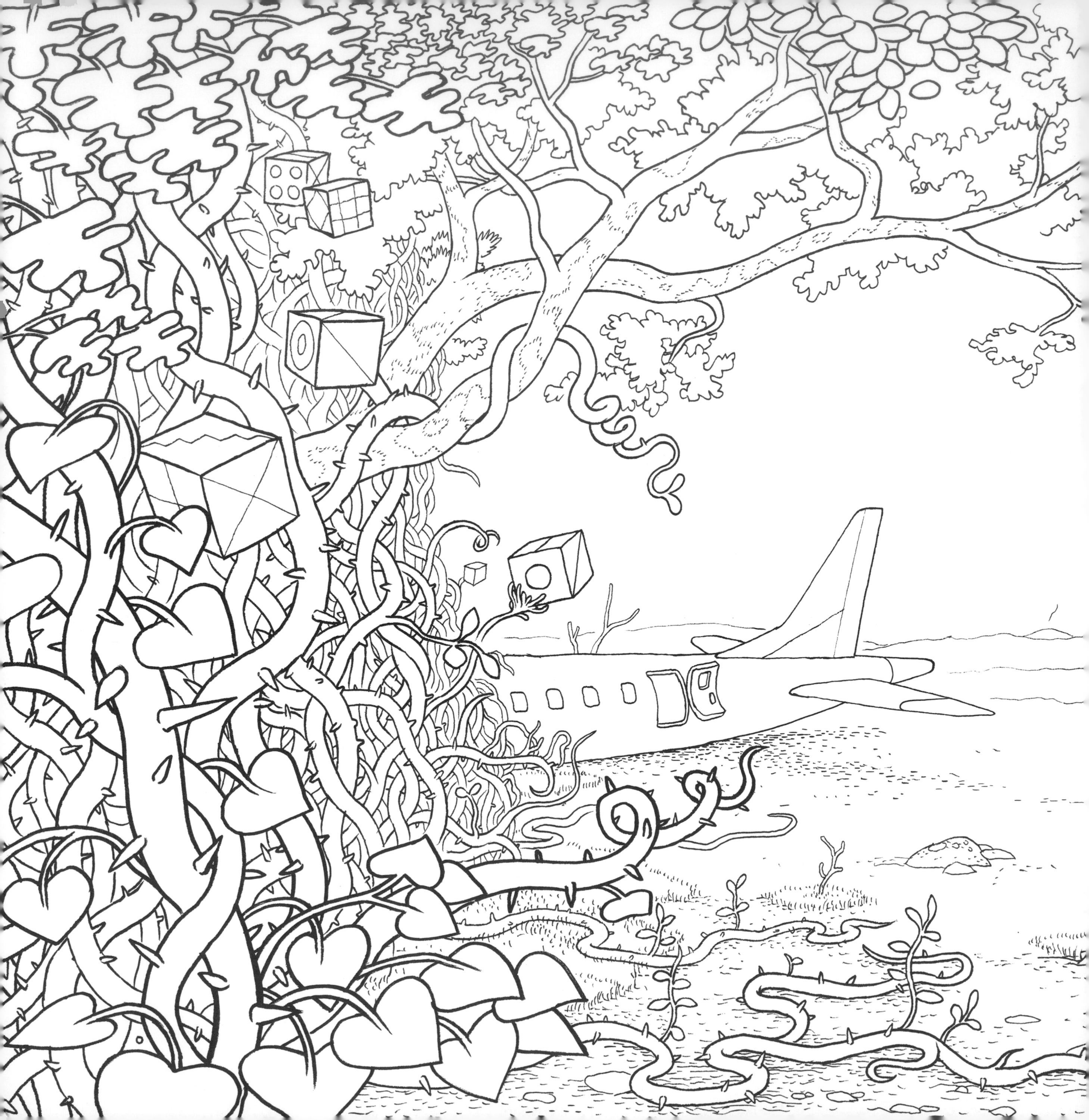

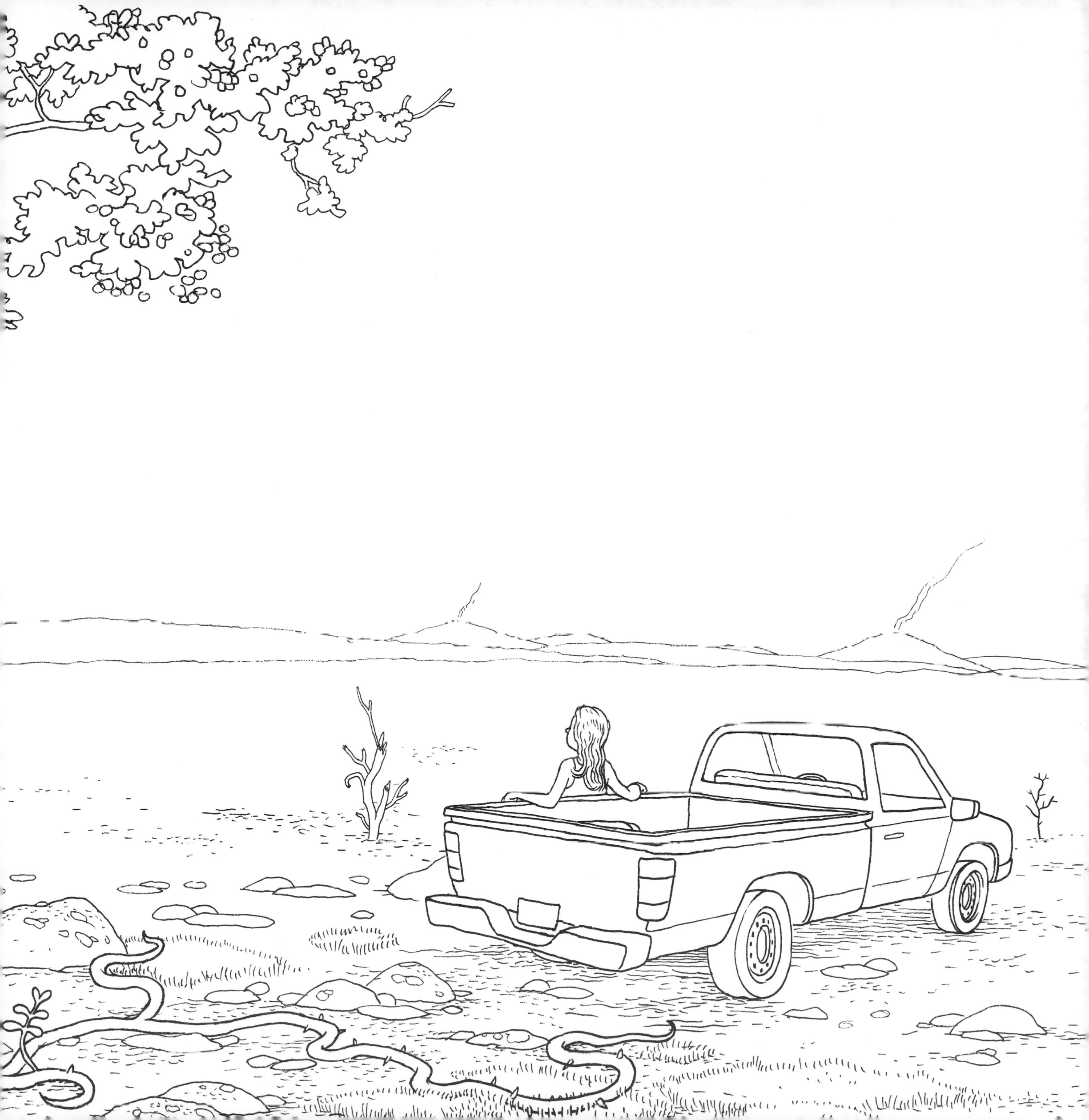

Some Things to Look for In and Around the Garden

- ☐ Adam
- ☐ Air Conditioner
- ☐ Airplane
- ☐ Antelopes
- ☐ Automobile
- ☐ Beach Ball
- ☐ Billboard
- ☐ Book
- ☐ Brontosaurus
- ☐ Cacti
- ☐ Cats
- ☐ Centaur
- ☐ Cerberus
- ☐ Coral
- ☐ Crystal Formations
- ☐ Dandelions
- ☐ Dodecahedron
- ☐ Dog, Explosive Mushroom Headed
- ☐ Dog, Patchy
- ☐ Dog, Shaggy
- ☐ Dog, Striped
- ☐ Dog Toy
- ☐ Ducks
- ☐ Egret
- ☐ Elephant
- ☐ Eve
- ☐ Fire Hydrant
- ☐ Fish-Man
- ☐ Flowers
- ☐ Fruit
- ☐ Giant Baby
- ☐ Giraffes
- ☐ God
- ☐ Gummy Angels
- ☐ Honda CB 125S
- ☐ Iced Latte
- ☐ Icosahedron
- ☐ Iguanas
- ☐ Jellyfish
- ☐ Ladder
- ☐ Lilith
- ☐ Mobile Home
- ☐ Monkeys
- ☐ Moon Rocket
- ☐ Moths
- ☐ Orangutan
- ☐ Ostriches
- ☐ Palm Trees
- ☐ Pay Phone
- ☐ Pickup Truck
- ☐ Piglet
- ☐ Pine Tree
- ☐ Puzzle Horse
- ☐ Rhinoceros
- ☐ Roses
- ☐ Seed Pod
- ☐ Sea Lions
- ☐ Sea Anemones
- ☐ Serpent
- ☐ Shellfish
- ☐ Soda Cup
- ☐ Striped Craters
- ☐ Tapir
- ☐ Telephones
- ☐ Thorny Hedge
- ☐ Tire
- ☐ Toad
- ☐ Topiary
- ☐ Toy Car
- ☐ Toy Pony
- ☐ Tree of the Knowledge of Good and Evil
- ☐ Triceratops
- ☐ Turtle
- ☐ Unicorn
- ☐ Volcanoes
- ☐ Warthogs